I0008296

Content Writing

A beginners guide to Effective Writing for Creating Engaging and SEO-Friendly Content for Websites, Blogs, and Social Media Platforms to Drive Traffic and Conversions

Heinrich Brevis

Copyright 2024 by Heinrich Brevis - All rights reserved.

This document is geared towards providing exact and reliable information in regards to the topic and issue covered. The publication is sold with the idea that the publisher is not required to render accounting, officially permitted, or otherwise, qualified services. If advice is necessary, legal or professional, a practiced individual in the profession should be ordered.

- From a Declaration of Principles which was accepted and approved equally by a Committee of the American Bar Association and a Committee of Publishers and Associations.

In no way is it legal to reproduce, duplicate, or transmit any part of this document in either electronic means or in printed format. Recording of this publication is strictly prohibited and any storage of this document is not allowed unless with written permission from the publisher. All rights reserved.

The information provided herein is stated to be truthful and consistent, in that any liability, in terms of inattention or otherwise, by any usage or abuse of any policies, processes, or directions contained within is the solitary and utter responsibility of the recipient reader. Under no circumstances will any legal responsibility or blame be held against the publisher for any reparation, damages, or monetary loss due to the information herein, either directly or indirectly.

Respective authors own all copyrights not held by the publisher.

The information herein is offered for informational purposes solely, and is universal as so.

The presentation of the information is without contract or any type of guarantee assurance.

The trademarks that are used are without any consent, and the publication of the trademark is without permission or backing by the trademark owner. All trademarks and brands within this book are for clarifying purposes only and are the owned by the owners themselves, not affiliated with this document

Table of Contents

Introduction

Welcome to "Content Writing: A Beginner's Guide to Effective Writing for Creating Engaging and SEO-Friendly Content for Websites, Blogs, and Social Media Platforms to Drive Traffic and Conversions." In today's digital age, content is the lifeblood of online communication and marketing. Whether you're a small business owner, an aspiring blogger, or a social media enthusiast, mastering the art of content writing is essential for establishing a strong online presence and achieving your goals.

The Power of Content

Content is more than just words on a screen; it's a powerful tool that can inform, entertain, and persuade. Quality content helps you connect with your audience, build trust, and establish authority in your niche. It is the cornerstone of effective digital marketing strategies, driving traffic to your website, engaging your audience on social media, and ultimately converting visitors into loyal customers.

Why This Guide?

The world of content writing can seem overwhelming, especially for beginners. With so much information available, it can be challenging to know where to start. This guide is designed to simplify the process, providing you with clear, actionable steps to create compelling content that resonates with your audience and performs well in search engines.

What You'll Learn

- **Fundamentals of Content Writing**: Understand the basics of content writing, including the importance of audience research, the elements of good writing, and the different types of content you can create.
- **SEO Essentials**: Learn how to optimize your content for search engines to improve visibility and drive organic traffic. This includes keyword research, on-page SEO techniques, and the importance of high-quality backlinks.
- **Creating Engaging Content**: Discover how to craft engaging and shareable content that captures the attention of your readers and encourages interaction. This section covers storytelling techniques, writing compelling headlines, and the use of visuals.
- **Writing for Different Platforms**: Explore the nuances of writing for various platforms, including websites, blogs, and social media. Each platform has its own set of best practices, and understanding these will help you maximize your reach and impact.
- **Driving Conversions**: Learn strategies to turn your content into a conversion tool. This includes writing persuasive calls to action, understanding the buyer's journey, and using content to nurture leads and drive sales.

The Journey Ahead

Embarking on the journey to becoming an effective content writer is both exciting and rewarding. With dedication and practice, you can develop the skills needed to create content that not only attracts and engages but also converts. This guide will serve as your roadmap, providing you with the knowledge and tools to succeed in the dynamic world of digital content writing.

As you dive into the chapters ahead, remember that content writing is both an art and a science. It requires creativity, analytical thinking, and a deep understanding of your audience. Whether you're writing a blog post, crafting a social media update, or optimizing your website content, each piece you create brings you one step closer to achieving your digital marketing goals.

Let's get started on your journey to becoming a skilled content writer, ready to make an impact in the digital world.

Chapter 1: Introduction to Content Writing

Content writing is the process of planning, creating, and publishing written material for various digital platforms. This includes websites, blogs, social media, emails, and other forms of online communication. The primary goal of content writing is to convey information in a way that is engaging, informative, and useful to the audience. Effective content writing goes beyond simply putting words together; it involves crafting messages that resonate with readers and inspire them to take action.

The Importance of Content Writing

In the digital landscape, content is a key driver of success. Here's why content writing is essential:

- **Building Relationships**: High-quality content helps establish a connection with your audience. It allows you to communicate your brand's voice, values, and personality, fostering trust and loyalty.
- **Driving Traffic**: Well-written, optimized content improves your search engine rankings, making it easier for potential customers to find you. More traffic means more opportunities for engagement and conversion.
- **Enhancing Engagement**: Engaging content captures the reader's attention and encourages them to interact with your brand. This can lead to increased time spent on your site, more shares on social media, and a stronger community around your brand.
- **Generating Leads and Conversions**: Persuasive content guides your audience through the buyer's journey, from awareness to

decision-making. Effective calls to action (CTAs) and informative content can turn casual readers into paying customers.

- **Establishing Authority**: By consistently providing valuable information, you can position yourself as an expert in your field. This authority can lead to greater trust from your audience and influence within your industry.

Key Elements of Effective Content Writing

To create content that achieves these goals, several key elements must be considered:

- **Audience Understanding**: Know who you are writing for. Understanding your audience's needs, preferences, and pain points is crucial for creating content that resonates.
- **Clarity and Simplicity**: Clear and concise writing is more effective than complicated prose. Aim to communicate your message in a straightforward and easy-to-understand manner.
- **Engagement**: Use storytelling techniques, interesting facts, and a conversational tone to keep readers engaged. Ask questions, invite comments, and encourage interaction.
- **SEO Optimization**: Incorporate relevant keywords naturally into your content to improve its visibility on search engines. SEO best practices help ensure that your content reaches a wider audience.
- **Originality**: Provide unique insights and perspectives. Original content stands out in a crowded digital space and adds value to your audience.

- **Consistency**: Regularly publishing content helps maintain audience interest and improves your site's SEO. Consistency in voice and style also strengthens brand identity.

Types of Content

Content writing encompasses various forms, each serving different purposes:

- **Blog Posts**: Informative articles that provide value to readers, often used to attract organic traffic and engage audiences.
- **Website Content**: Pages like the homepage, about us, services, and product descriptions that convey essential information about your business.
- **Social Media Posts**: Short, engaging updates that drive interaction and promote content across platforms like Facebook, Twitter, and Instagram.
- **Email Newsletters**: Regular emails that keep your audience informed about updates, offers, and valuable content.
- **Whitepapers and E-books**: In-depth guides that provide detailed information on a specific topic, often used for lead generation.
- **Case Studies and Testimonials**: Real-life examples that showcase your success and build credibility.

The Content Writing Process

Creating effective content involves several steps:

- **Research**: Gather information about your topic, audience, and competitors. Use reliable sources to ensure accuracy.
- **Planning**: Outline your content, defining the main points and structure. A clear plan helps maintain focus and coherence.
- **Writing**: Draft your content, focusing on clarity, engagement, and SEO optimization. Write in a natural and conversational tone.
- **Editing and Proofreading**: Review your content for errors, consistency, and readability. Editing ensures your message is clear and polished.
- **Publishing**: Post your content on the appropriate platforms. Use appealing visuals and headlines to attract attention.
- **Promotion**: Share your content through social media, email, and other channels to reach a wider audience.
- **Analysis and Improvement**: Monitor the performance of your content. Use analytics to understand what works and refine your strategy accordingly.

Content writing is a vital skill in the digital age, offering numerous benefits from increased traffic to higher engagement and conversions. By understanding the fundamentals and applying best practices, you can create content that not only captivates your audience but also drives meaningful results for your brand. As we delve deeper into this guide, you'll gain the tools and knowledge to master the art of content writing and harness its full potential for your digital endeavors.

1.1 What is Content Writing?

Content writing is the process of creating written material that serves various purposes in the digital realm. It involves crafting text that is not only informative and engaging but also tailored to meet the needs of a specific audience. Content writing encompasses a broad range of formats, including blog posts, website pages, and social media updates, emails, whitepapers, and more.

The Essence of Content Writing

At its core, content writing is about communication. It aims to convey a message, tell a story, or provide information in a way that captures the reader's interest and fulfills their needs. Effective content writing requires a deep understanding of the audience, a clear purpose, and a structured approach to presenting information.

Key Objectives of Content Writing

- **Informing**: Providing valuable and relevant information that educates the audience on a particular topic. This can range from how-to guides and tutorials to detailed analyses and reports.
- **Engaging**: Capturing the reader's attention and keeping them interested throughout the piece. Engaging content often includes elements like storytelling, interesting facts, and a conversational tone.
- **Persuading**: Encouraging readers to take a specific action, such as making a purchase, signing up for a newsletter, or sharing the content on social media. Persuasive content includes strong calls to action and compelling arguments.
- **Entertaining**: Providing enjoyment to the reader through humor, anecdotes, or creative storytelling. Entertaining content helps to build a connection with the audience and makes the content more memorable.

- **SEO (Search Engine Optimization)**: Ensuring that content is easily discoverable by search engines, thereby increasing its visibility and attracting organic traffic. This involves the strategic use of keywords, meta descriptions, and other SEO techniques.

Types of Content Writing

Content writing can take many forms, each with its own style and purpose:

- **Blog Posts**: These are articles published on a blog, typically informative and designed to attract organic traffic through SEO. Blog posts can range from personal reflections to in-depth guides.
- **Website Content**: This includes the text found on a company's website, such as the homepage, about us page, product descriptions, and service pages. It aims to provide clear and concise information about the business and its offerings.
- **Social Media Content**: Short and engaging posts tailored for platforms like Facebook, Twitter, Instagram, and LinkedIn. The goal is to foster interaction and shareability.
- **Email Newsletters**: Regular emails sent to subscribers with updates, offers, and valuable content. The focus is on maintaining a relationship with the audience and driving conversions.
- **Whitepapers and E-books**: Long-form content that provides detailed insights into a specific topic. These are often used for lead generation and to establish authority in a particular field.
- **Case Studies and Testimonials**: Real-life examples and success stories that showcase the effectiveness of a product or service. These build credibility and trust with potential customers.

The Content Writing Process

Creating high-quality content involves several steps:

- **Research**: Understanding the topic thoroughly and gathering relevant information. This includes studying the target audience, analyzing competitors, and identifying key points to cover.
- **Planning**: Outlining the structure of the content. This involves deciding on the main points, the flow of information, and how to present the content logically and engagingly.
- **Writing**: Crafting the content itself, focusing on clarity, readability, and engagement. It's important to write in a tone that resonates with the audience and aligns with the brand's voice.
- **Editing and Proofreading**: Reviewing the content to correct errors, ensure consistency, and improve overall quality. This step is crucial for producing polished and professional content.
- **Publishing**: Posting the content on the appropriate platform, whether it's a blog, website, or social media channel. This may also involve adding visuals, formatting, and optimizing for SEO.
- **Promotion**: Sharing the content through various channels to reach a wider audience. This includes social media promotion, email marketing, and collaborations with influencers or other websites.
- **Analysis and Improvement**: Monitoring the performance of the content using analytics tools. This helps to understand what works, what doesn't, and how to improve future content.

Content writing is a multifaceted discipline that plays a crucial role in digital communication and marketing. By understanding its principles and applying best practices, you can create content that not only informs and engages but also drives meaningful results for your brand or business. Whether you're writing a blog post, crafting a social media update, or developing an email newsletter, effective content writing can help you connect with your audience and achieve your objectives.

1.2 Importance of Quality Content

In the vast digital landscape, where countless voices compete for attention, the importance of quality content cannot be overstated. High-quality content is the cornerstone of successful online communication and marketing. It plays a crucial role in attracting, engaging, and retaining audiences, ultimately driving business success. Let's delve into why quality content is so essential.

Building Trust and Credibility

Quality content helps establish trust and credibility with your audience. When you consistently provide valuable, accurate, and well-researched information, readers are more likely to view you as an authority in your field. This trust is fundamental for building long-term relationships with your audience, which can lead to increased loyalty and customer retention.

Enhancing User Experience

High-quality content enhances the user experience by providing relevant and engaging information that meets the needs and interests of your audience. Well-structured, easy-to-read content keeps readers on your site longer, reduces bounce rates, and encourages them to explore more of your offerings. A positive user experience can lead to higher conversion rates and better overall performance for your digital platforms.

Improving SEO and Visibility

Search engines like Google prioritize high-quality content in their rankings. By producing well-optimized, informative content, you can improve your website's search engine visibility, attracting more organic traffic. Key factors that contribute to SEO include the use of relevant keywords, informative headings, internal and external links, and the overall readability of your content. Quality content not only helps you rank higher but also ensures that visitors find your site valuable and worth returning to.

Driving Engagement and Social Shares

Engaging content resonates with readers, prompting them to interact, comment, and share it with their networks. This social sharing amplifies your reach and can drive significant traffic to your site. Content that sparks conversations and encourages user-generated content further boosts engagement and helps build a community around your brand.

Supporting Lead Generation and Conversions

Quality content is a powerful tool for lead generation and conversions. Informative blog posts, in-depth whitepapers, and compelling case studies can attract potential customers and guide them through the buyer's journey. By addressing pain points, answering questions, and providing solutions, quality content can persuade readers to take the next step, whether it's signing up for a newsletter, requesting a quote, or making a purchase.

Establishing Brand Voice and Identity

Consistent, high-quality content helps define and reinforce your brand voice and identity. It allows you to communicate your brand's values, mission, and personality effectively. A strong brand identity, supported by quality content, differentiates you from competitors and makes your brand more memorable to your audience.

Providing Value Beyond the Sale

Quality content offers value beyond just promoting products or services. It educates, entertains, and informs your audience, building a deeper connection with them. By focusing on delivering value, you position your brand as a trusted resource that readers can turn to, even when they are not in the buying phase.

Adapting to Changing Trends and Needs

In a rapidly evolving digital world, staying relevant is crucial. Quality content allows you to adapt to changing trends and audience needs. By keeping up with industry developments and addressing current topics, you can ensure that your content remains timely and valuable, keeping your audience engaged and informed.

The importance of quality content in digital marketing and communication cannot be underestimated. It builds trust, enhances user experience, improves SEO, drives engagement, supports lead generation, establishes brand identity, provides ongoing value, and helps you stay relevant. By investing time and effort into creating high-quality content, you lay a solid foundation for achieving your business goals and fostering a loyal, engaged audience. As you continue through this guide, you'll learn more about how to create content that meets these high standards and drives meaningful results for your brand.

1.3 The Role of Content in Digital Marketing

In the digital marketing ecosystem, content is not just king—it's the entire kingdom. Content serves as the foundation upon which all digital marketing strategies are built. Whether you are looking to increase brand awareness, drive traffic, generate leads, or boost conversions, content is at the heart of it all. Understanding the multifaceted role of content in digital marketing is essential for creating effective strategies that deliver results.

Driving Traffic

One of the primary roles of content in digital marketing is to attract visitors to your website. High-quality, optimized content helps improve your site's search engine rankings, making it easier for potential customers to find you. Blog posts, articles, videos, infographics, and other content types can be tailored to target specific keywords and topics that your audience is searching for, driving organic traffic to your site.

Engaging Your Audience

Content is crucial for engaging your audience. It allows you to capture their attention, provide valuable information, and keep them coming back for more. Engaging content, such as compelling blog posts, interactive videos, and insightful social media updates, encourages readers to spend more time on your site and interact with your brand. This increased engagement can lead to higher conversion rates and stronger customer relationships.

Building Brand Awareness and Authority

Through consistent and high-quality content, you can build brand awareness and establish your authority in your industry. Content that educates, informs, and solves problems for your audience positions your brand as a trusted source of information. This credibility helps attract more visitors, earn trust, and build a loyal following. Over time, your brand becomes synonymous with expertise and reliability in your niche.

Supporting SEO Efforts

Content and SEO go hand in hand. Search engines favor websites that offer valuable, relevant, and regularly updated content. By incorporating SEO best practices into your content creation process—such as keyword optimization, meta descriptions, and internal linking—you can improve your site's visibility on search engine results pages (SERPs). This increased visibility drives more organic traffic to your site, enhancing your overall digital marketing efforts.

Generating Leads

Content is a powerful tool for lead generation. By offering valuable resources such as e-books, whitepapers, webinars, and case studies, you can attract potential customers and capture their information through lead magnets and opt-in forms. Once you have their contact information, you can nurture these leads with targeted content and personalized follow-up emails, guiding them through the sales funnel.

Nurturing and Converting Leads

Effective content marketing doesn't stop at lead generation; it also involves nurturing and converting leads into customers. Through email marketing, drip campaigns, and personalized content, you can provide leads with the information they need at each stage of the buyer's journey. Educational blog posts, product guides, customer testimonials, and other targeted content help address their concerns and persuade them to make a purchase.

Enhancing Social Media Presence

Content fuels your social media marketing efforts. Regularly sharing valuable and engaging content on social media platforms helps you connect with your audience, increase your reach, and drive traffic back to your website. Social media also allows for real-time interaction with your audience, providing opportunities for engagement, feedback, and building community around your brand.

Supporting Paid Advertising

Content is essential for effective paid advertising campaigns. Whether you're running pay-per-click (PPC) ads, social media ads, or display ads, the quality of your content determines the success of your campaigns. Compelling ad copy, informative landing pages, and engaging video content can significantly improve your ad performance, leading to higher click-through rates (CTR) and conversions.

Measuring and Analyzing Performance

Content provides valuable data that can be used to measure and analyze the performance of your digital marketing efforts. By tracking metrics such as page views, time on site, bounce rate, social shares, and conversion rates, you can gain insights into what content resonates with your audience and what needs improvement. This data-driven approach helps you refine your content strategy and achieve better results over time.

Content plays a pivotal role in digital marketing, influencing every aspect of your strategy from attracting traffic and engaging your audience to generating leads and driving conversions. High-quality, relevant content is the backbone of effective digital marketing, enabling you to build brand awareness, establish authority, and connect with your audience on a deeper level. As you continue to develop your content marketing skills, remember that the key to success lies in creating value for your audience and consistently delivering content that meets their needs and exceeds their expectations.

1.4 Understanding Different Content Platforms

In the digital landscape, content platforms are the various channels through which you can publish and share your content. Each platform has its unique characteristics, audience, and best practices. Understanding these differences is crucial for creating content that resonates with your target audience and achieves your marketing goals. In this section, we'll explore some of the most popular content platforms and how to leverage them effectively.

Websites

Websites are the central hub of your online presence. They serve as the primary platform for hosting a wide range of content, including blog posts, product pages, service descriptions, and more. Key considerations for website content include:

- **SEO Optimization**: Incorporate relevant keywords, meta tags, and structured data to improve search engine rankings.
- **User Experience**: Ensure your website is easy to navigate, mobile-friendly, and fast-loading.
- **Engaging Copy**: Write clear, concise, and compelling copy that addresses the needs and interests of your audience.

Blogs

Blogs are a crucial component of content marketing. They provide a platform for sharing in-depth articles, how-to guides, industry insights, and other valuable content. Blogs help establish authority, drive organic traffic, and engage readers. Best practices for blogging include:

- **Consistent Posting**: Regularly publish new posts to keep your audience engaged and improve SEO.
- **Quality Over Quantity**: Focus on providing valuable, well-researched content rather than just frequent updates.
- **Interactive Elements**: Include images, videos, infographics, and interactive content to enhance reader engagement.

Social Media

Social media platforms like Facebook, Twitter, Instagram, LinkedIn, and Pinterest are essential for reaching a broad audience and fostering engagement. Each platform has its unique features and user demographics:

- **Facebook**: Great for sharing a mix of content types, including articles, videos, and community posts. Use Facebook Ads to target specific audiences.
- **Twitter**: Ideal for real-time updates, news, and short-form content. Use hashtags to increase visibility and engagement.
- **Instagram**: Focuses on visual content like photos and videos. Utilize Stories, Reels, and IGTV for varied content formats.
- **LinkedIn**: Best for professional and B2B content. Share industry insights, case studies, and thought leadership articles.
- **Pinterest**: Visual discovery platform ideal for lifestyle, DIY, and e-commerce content. Use pins and boards to organize and share content.

Email Newsletters

Email newsletters are an effective way to nurture relationships with your audience, keep them informed, and drive traffic to your website. Key strategies for email newsletters include:

- **Personalization**: Customize content based on subscriber preferences and behaviors.
- **Compelling Subject Lines**: Write catchy and relevant subject lines to increase open rates.
- **Value-Driven Content**: Provide exclusive insights, offers, and updates that are valuable to your subscribers.

Video Platforms

Video platforms like YouTube, Vimeo, and TikTok are powerful tools for engaging audiences with visual and auditory content. Videos can explain complex topics, showcase products, and tell compelling stories. Tips for video content include:

- **High-Quality Production**: Ensure good video and audio quality to maintain a professional image.
- **SEO for Videos**: Optimize titles, descriptions, and tags with relevant keywords.
- **Engaging Thumbnails**: Use attractive and relevant thumbnails to increase click-through rates.

Podcasts

Podcasts are an increasingly popular medium for sharing long-form content in an audio format. They are great for storytelling, interviews, and in-depth discussions. To create successful podcasts:

- **Consistent Schedule**: Release episodes on a regular schedule to build a loyal audience.
- **Engaging Content**: Focus on topics that are relevant and interesting to your target audience.
- **Professional Quality**: Invest in good recording equipment and editing software to produce high-quality audio.

Webinars and Live Streams

Webinars and live streams provide a platform for real-time interaction with your audience. They are ideal for demonstrations, Q&A sessions, and interactive presentations. Best practices include:

- **Promotion**: Promote your webinar or live stream in advance through multiple channels.
- **Engagement**: Encourage audience participation through polls, questions, and live chat.
- **Follow-Up**: Send follow-up emails with recordings and additional resources to attendees.

Each content platform offers unique opportunities and requires specific strategies to maximize its potential. By understanding the strengths and best practices of different platforms, you can create a diversified content strategy that reaches and engages your target audience effectively. As you continue to develop your content marketing skills, remember to tailor your content to fit the platform and audience, ensuring that your message is both impactful and relevant.

1.5 Key Skills for Effective Content Writing

Effective content writing requires a diverse set of skills that go beyond simply being able to write well. To create compelling, engaging, and SEO-friendly content that resonates with your audience and achieves your marketing goals, you need to develop and refine several key abilities. Here are the essential skills every content writer should master:

Research Skills

Research is the foundation of high-quality content. Effective content writers must be adept at:

- **Finding Reliable Sources**: Identify and use credible sources to gather accurate information. This includes academic journals, industry reports, reputable websites, and expert interviews.
- **Understanding the Topic**: Gain a deep understanding of the subject matter to write confidently and authoritatively.
- **Audience Research**: Know your target audience's needs, preferences, and pain points to tailor your content accordingly.

SEO Knowledge

Search Engine Optimization (SEO) is critical for increasing the visibility of your content. Key SEO skills include:

- **Keyword Research**: Identify relevant keywords and phrases that your audience is searching for and incorporate them naturally into your content.
- **On-Page SEO**: Optimize elements such as meta titles, descriptions, headers, and images to improve search engine rankings.
- **Content Structure**: Use clear headings, subheadings, and bullet points to make your content more readable and search engine-friendly.

Writing and Grammar

Strong writing skills are a must for any content writer. This includes:

- **Clarity and Conciseness**: Write clear and concise content that is easy to understand.
- **Grammar and Punctuation**: Use proper grammar, punctuation, and spelling to maintain professionalism and readability.
- **Variety in Sentence Structure**: Use a mix of short and long sentences to keep the reader engaged and the content flowing smoothly.

Adaptability

Content writers must be able to adapt their writing style to different formats and platforms. This involves:

- **Understanding Different Tones**: Write in a tone that suits the platform and audience, whether it's formal, conversational, humorous, or authoritative.
- **Content Types**: Be versatile in creating various types of content, such as blog posts, social media updates, email newsletters, whitepapers, and more.
- **Adjusting Length and Depth**: Tailor the length and depth of content to match the platform and audience's expectations.

Creativity

Creativity is essential for making your content stand out. This includes:

- **Unique Perspectives**: Offer fresh insights and unique angles on familiar topics.
- **Storytelling**: Use storytelling techniques to make your content more engaging and relatable.
- **Visual Content**: Incorporate images, infographics, videos, and other visual elements to enhance the reader's experience.

Editing and Proofreading

Editing and proofreading are crucial for producing polished content. Key skills include:

- **Attention to Detail**: Spot and correct errors in grammar, punctuation, spelling, and formatting.
- **Consistency**: Ensure consistency in tone, style, and voice throughout the content.
- **Clarity**: Simplify complex ideas and eliminate unnecessary jargon to make the content more accessible.

Time Management

Content writers often work on multiple projects with tight deadlines. Effective time management involves:

- **Prioritization**: Identify the most important tasks and tackle them first.
- **Scheduling**: Allocate specific times for research, writing, editing, and breaks to maintain productivity.
- **Meeting Deadlines**: Deliver high-quality content on time, every time.

Communication Skills

Strong communication skills are essential for collaborating with clients, editors, and other team members. This includes:

- **Active Listening**: Understand the requirements and expectations of your clients or stakeholders.
- **Clear Expression**: Communicate your ideas, suggestions, and concerns effectively.
- **Feedback Handling**: Accept and implement feedback constructively to improve your work.

Analytical Thinking

Analytical skills help you evaluate the effectiveness of your content and make data-driven decisions. This involves:

- **Performance Analysis**: Use analytics tools to track metrics such as page views, time on site, bounce rates, and conversion rates.
- **Content Optimization**: Identify areas for improvement and optimize content based on performance data.
- **Audience Insights**: Analyze audience behavior and feedback to refine your content strategy.

Mastering these key skills will enable you to create content that is not only well-written but also effective in achieving your marketing objectives. As you continue to develop your content writing abilities, focus on honing each of these skills to become a versatile and successful content writer. Remember that content writing is both an art and a science, requiring creativity, technical knowledge, and strategic thinking to truly excel.

Chapter 2: Understanding Your Audience

Creating compelling content begins with a deep understanding of your audience. Knowing who your audience is, what they need, and how they interact with content is crucial for crafting messages that resonate and drive engagement. In this chapter, we will explore the importance of understanding your audience and how to gather and apply audience insights to enhance your content strategy.

Understanding your audience is the foundation of any successful content strategy. When you know your audience well, you can tailor your content to address their specific needs, preferences, and pain points. This customization increases engagement, as you create content that captures attention and encourages interaction. A deep understanding of your audience also helps in building trust. By showing that you understand and care about their interests, you establish a deeper connection, which is crucial for fostering loyalty and driving conversions. When your audience feels understood, they are more likely to take desired actions, such as subscribing to a newsletter, downloading a resource, or making a purchase.

Identifying your target audience involves understanding the demographic, psychographic, and behavioral characteristics of the people you want to reach. Demographic analysis gathers data on age, gender, income, education, occupation, and location to define the basic characteristics of your audience. Psychographic analysis explores the interests, values, attitudes, and lifestyle choices of your audience to gain deeper insights into their motivations and preferences. Behavioral analysis studies the online behavior of your audience, including their content consumption patterns, purchasing behavior, and interaction with your brand. Together, these analyses provide a comprehensive picture of your target audience.

Creating buyer personas is a practical way to visualize and understand your audience better. Buyer personas are semi-fictional representations of your ideal customers based on data and insights. To create effective buyer personas, you should start with thorough research. Use surveys, interviews, and data analysis to gather detailed information about your audience. Next, segment your audience into distinct groups based on common characteristics and behaviors. Finally, develop detailed profiles for each persona, including name, background, demographics, goals, challenges, and preferences. These profiles help you tailor your content to meet the specific needs of each audience segment.

Analyzing audience data is crucial for refining your content strategy and making informed decisions. Web analytics tools like Google Analytics can track website traffic, user behavior, and conversion rates, providing valuable insights into how your audience interacts with your content. Social media insights offer metrics such as likes, shares, comments, and follower demographics, helping you understand your audience's engagement and preferences. Content performance metrics, including page views, time on page, bounce rates, and click-through rates, allow you to evaluate the effectiveness of your content and identify areas for improvement.

Listening to your audience involves actively seeking and considering their feedback and opinions. Conducting surveys and polls is a direct way to gather feedback on your content and brand. Monitoring and responding to comments and reviews on your website, blog, and social media channels provides real-time insights into how your audience perceives your content. Engaging with online communities, forums, and groups where your audience is active allows you to understand their discussions and concerns, helping you create content that truly resonates with them.

Applying audience insights to your content strategy involves several key steps. Develop a content calendar that aligns with your audience's interests, preferences, and seasonal trends. Create personalized content that addresses the specific needs and interests of different audience segments. Continuously optimize your content based on performance data and audience feedback to improve its effectiveness. By incorporating these insights into your content strategy, you can create more relevant, engaging, and effective content.

Understanding your audience is a continuous process that requires ongoing research, analysis, and adaptation. By gaining a deep understanding of who your audience is and what they want, you can create content that resonates, engages, and drives meaningful results. In the next chapters, we will explore how to apply these audience insights to craft compelling content and optimize your content strategy for maximum impact.

2.1 Identifying Your Target Audience

Identifying your target audience is a critical first step in developing a successful content strategy. It involves understanding the demographic, psychographic, and behavioral characteristics of the individuals or groups you aim to reach with your content. By defining your target audience clearly, you can create content that resonates deeply and effectively addresses their needs and preferences.

Demographic Analysis

Demographic analysis focuses on quantifiable characteristics of your audience, including age, gender, income level, education, occupation, marital status, and geographic location. These factors provide foundational insights into who your potential audience members are and help you segment your target audience accordingly.

Psychographic Analysis

Psychographic analysis delves into the psychological and social factors that influence your audience's behaviors, preferences, values, beliefs, interests, and lifestyle choices. This analysis goes beyond demographics to uncover the motivations and aspirations that drive consumer decisions and content consumption habits.

Behavioral Analysis

Behavioral analysis examines how your audience interacts with content, products, services, and brands online. It includes understanding their browsing habits, purchase patterns, content consumption preferences (such as preferred formats and topics), social media usage, and engagement with online communities. Behavioral data provides insights into the actions your audience takes and helps tailor your content to better meet their expectations.

By conducting thorough demographic, psychographic, and behavioral analyses, you can create detailed profiles or personas of your target audience segments. These personas serve as fictional representations that embody the characteristics, behaviors, needs, and goals of your ideal customers or audience members. Developing clear and detailed personas enables you to tailor your content strategy more effectively, ensuring that your messaging resonates with and engages your target audience on a deeper level.

Understanding your target audience is an ongoing process that requires continuous monitoring and adjustment as consumer behaviors and market trends evolve. By regularly revisiting and refining your audience insights, you can optimize your content strategy to maintain relevance, maximize engagement, and achieve your marketing objectives effectively.

2.2 Creating Audience Personas

Audience personas, also known as buyer personas, are fictional representations of your ideal customers based on research and data about your real audience segments. These personas help you understand your target audience on a deeper level and guide your content strategy by aligning it with their needs, preferences, and behaviors.

Why Create Audience Personas?

Creating audience personas is essential for several reasons:

- **Focus and Clarity**: Personas provide a clear and focused picture of who your target audience is, including their demographics, motivations, challenges, and goals.
- **Tailored Content**: With personas, you can tailor your content to address specific pain points, interests, and preferences of different audience segments.
- **Improved Marketing Strategies**: Personas enable you to develop more effective marketing strategies by aligning your messaging and tactics with the needs and behaviors of your target audience.

- **Better Customer Understanding**: Understanding your audience through personas helps build empathy and deeper connections with your customers, leading to improved customer satisfaction and loyalty.

Steps to Create Audience Personas

Creating effective audience personas involves the following steps:

- **Research**: Gather data from various sources, including surveys, interviews, customer feedback, and analytics tools. Focus on demographic information, psychographic insights, and behavioral patterns.
- **Identify Patterns**: Analyze the data to identify common characteristics and behaviors among your audience segments. Look for trends, preferences, and pain points that can inform your personas.
- **Segmentation**: Group your audience into distinct segments based on shared characteristics and behaviors. This segmentation helps you create specific personas that represent different subsets of your target audience.
- **Persona Development**: Develop detailed profiles for each persona, including:
- **Demographics**: Age, gender, income, education, occupation, geographic location.
- **Psychographics**: Interests, values, attitudes, lifestyle choices, aspirations.
- **Behaviors**: Content consumption habits, purchasing behaviors, preferred channels.

- **Goals and Challenges**: What they aim to achieve and what obstacles they face.
- **Persona Naming and Visualization**: Give each persona a name and create a visual representation, such as a photo or illustration. This makes the persona more relatable and memorable for your team.

Using Audience Personas

Once you have created audience personas, use them to guide your content strategy in the following ways:

- **Content Creation**: Develop content ideas and formats that resonate with each persona's interests and preferences.
- **Messaging**: Tailor your messaging to address the specific needs, challenges, and aspirations of each persona.
- **Channel Selection**: Choose the most effective channels and platforms for reaching each persona based on their preferred content consumption habits.
- **Personalization**: Implement personalized marketing tactics that speak directly to the concerns and motivations of each persona.

Continuous Refinement

Audience personas should be dynamic and evolve as you gather more data and insights. Regularly update and refine your personas based on new information and changes in market trends or audience behaviors.

This ensures that your content remains relevant and resonates with your target audience effectively.

By investing time and effort into creating and utilizing audience personas, you can significantly enhance the relevance, engagement, and effectiveness of your content marketing efforts. Personas serve as invaluable tools for aligning your content strategy with the needs and preferences of your audience, ultimately driving better business outcomes and fostering stronger customer relationships.

2.3 Analyzing Audience Needs and Preferences

Analyzing audience needs and preferences is crucial for crafting content that resonates deeply with your target audience. By understanding what your audience wants, values, and expects from your content, you can tailor your messages to effectively meet their expectations and drive engagement. In this section, we'll explore how to analyze audience needs and preferences to inform your content strategy.

Gathering Data

Start by collecting data from various sources to gain insights into your audience's needs and preferences:

- **Surveys and Questionnaires**: Conduct surveys to directly ask your audience about their preferences, interests, and challenges.
- **Website Analytics**: Use tools like Google Analytics to track user behavior on your website, including page views, bounce rates, and time spent on pages.

- **Social Media Insights**: Analyze metrics such as likes, shares, comments, and follower demographics on social media platforms to understand audience engagement.
- **Customer Feedback**: Review feedback from customer support interactions, reviews, and comments to uncover common concerns and preferences.
- **Competitor Analysis**: Study your competitors to identify successful content strategies and audience preferences within your industry.

Identifying Patterns and Trends

Once you have gathered data, look for patterns and trends that indicate common preferences and needs among your audience:

- **Demographic Insights**: Identify demographic groups that show similar content consumption habits and preferences.
- **Content Interactions**: Analyze which types of content (e.g., blog posts, videos, infographics) receive the most engagement and resonate most with your audience.
- **Topic Preferences**: Determine which topics and themes generate the most interest and discussion among your audience.
- **Behavioral Analysis**: Study how your audience interacts with different types of content and channels, including preferred times of engagement and device usage patterns.

Understanding Motivations and Challenges

Dig deeper to understand the motivations and challenges that drive your audience's content consumption behaviors:

- **Goals**: Determine what goals your audience is trying to achieve and how your content can help them reach those goals.
- **Pain Points**: Identify common challenges or pain points that your audience faces and address them through your content.
- **Information Needs**: Assess what information gaps exist among your audience and create content that provides valuable insights and solutions.

Applying Insights to Content Strategy

Use the insights gathered from your analysis to inform and optimize your content strategy:

- **Content Planning**: Develop a content calendar that prioritizes topics and formats based on audience preferences and seasonal trends.
- **Content Creation**: Tailor your content to address specific needs, preferences, and pain points identified through your analysis.
- **Personalization**: Implement personalized content strategies that speak directly to different segments of your audience.
- **Optimization**: Continuously optimize your content based on audience feedback and performance metrics to enhance engagement and relevance.

Continuous Monitoring and Adjustment

Audience needs and preferences evolve, so it's essential to continuously monitor and adjust your content strategy:

- **Feedback Loop**: Establish a feedback loop to gather ongoing insights from your audience through surveys, social media listening, and customer interactions.
- **Analytics Review**: Regularly review analytics data to track changes in audience behavior and adjust your strategy accordingly.
- **Industry Trends**: Stay informed about industry trends and competitor activities to anticipate shifts in audience preferences and adapt proactively.

By systematically analyzing your audience's needs and preferences, you can create content that resonates deeply, drives engagement, and ultimately achieves your marketing goals. Effective content strategies are built on a foundation of audience understanding, ensuring that every piece of content you create is valuable, relevant, and impactful to your target audience.

2.4 Conducting Market Research

Market research is a critical process for gathering valuable insights into your target audience, competitors, industry trends, and market dynamics. It provides the foundation for developing informed strategies and making data-driven decisions to drive the success of your content marketing efforts. In this section, we will explore the key aspects and methods of conducting effective market research.

Importance of Market Research

Market research plays a pivotal role in shaping your content strategy by:

- **Understanding Audience Needs**: Identifying the preferences, behaviors, and pain points of your target audience to create relevant and engaging content.
- **Competitor Analysis**: Assessing competitor strategies, strengths, weaknesses, and market positioning to identify opportunities and differentiate your content offerings.
- **Industry Insights**: Staying informed about industry trends, emerging technologies, and regulatory changes that impact your target market.
- **Validation of Ideas**: Testing new content ideas, formats, and strategies to gauge potential success and mitigate risks.

Methods of Market Research

- **Surveys and Questionnaires**: Gather direct feedback from your audience to understand their preferences, interests, and satisfaction levels with your content and brand.
- **Focus Groups**: Conduct moderated discussions with small groups of representative audience members to explore opinions, perceptions, and deeper insights.

- **Interviews**: Conduct one-on-one interviews with key stakeholders, industry experts, or customers to gather qualitative insights and validate quantitative data.
- **Data Analysis**: Utilize tools like Google Analytics, social media analytics, and customer relationship management (CRM) systems to analyze user behavior, engagement metrics, and demographic data.
- **Competitor Analysis**: Study competitor content strategies, SEO tactics, social media presence, and customer feedback to identify strengths, weaknesses, and opportunities for differentiation.
- **Trend Analysis**: Monitor industry publications, market reports, and online discussions to identify emerging trends, consumer preferences, and technological advancements relevant to your market.

Steps in Market Research

- **Define Objectives**: Clearly outline your research goals, such as understanding audience preferences, identifying market gaps, or validating new content ideas.
- **Develop Research Plan**: Create a structured plan outlining the methods, tools, timeline, and resources required to conduct comprehensive market research.
- **Collect Data**: Execute your research plan by implementing selected methods to gather relevant data from primary (direct sources) and secondary (existing data) sources.
- **Analyze Findings**: Interpret and analyze collected data to identify patterns, trends, and actionable insights that inform your content strategy and decision-making.

- **Draw Conclusions**: Draw meaningful conclusions based on your analysis and determine strategic recommendations for optimizing content performance and market positioning.
- **Implement Insights**: Apply insights gained from market research to refine your content strategy, improve audience targeting, and enhance the effectiveness of your content marketing campaigns.

Continuous Improvement

Market research is an ongoing process that requires continuous monitoring and adaptation to changing market dynamics and audience preferences. Regularly revisit your research findings, update your understanding of the market landscape, and refine your strategies to stay ahead of competitors and meet evolving consumer expectations.

By conducting thorough market research, you empower your content marketing efforts with actionable insights that drive audience engagement, optimize resource allocation, and ultimately contribute to achieving your business objectives effectively.

2.5 Adapting Content to Audience Demographics

Adapting content to audience demographics is essential for creating targeted and impactful content strategies. Demographics such as age, gender, income, education, occupation, and geographic location provide valuable insights into the characteristics and preferences of your audience segments. By understanding these demographic factors and tailoring your content accordingly, you can enhance engagement, relevance, and effectiveness in reaching your target audience.

Understanding Audience Demographics

- **Age**: Different age groups have distinct preferences and behaviors when consuming content. For example, younger audiences may prefer short-form videos on social media, while older demographics might prefer in-depth articles or webinars.
- **Gender**: Gender can influence content preferences and perspectives. Understanding gender demographics helps in crafting messages that resonate with specific gender identities and avoid stereotypes.
- **Income**: Income levels affect purchasing power and consumer behavior. Tailoring content to income demographics involves offering relevant products or services and addressing financial considerations appropriately.
- **Education**: Education levels influence the complexity and depth of content that resonates with audiences. Highly educated audiences may appreciate detailed, research-driven content, whereas less educated audiences may prefer straightforward, easy-to-understand information.
- **Occupation**: Occupation can provide insights into professional interests and challenges. Content adapted to different occupations can address industry-specific needs and showcase relevant expertise.
- **Geographic Location**: Cultural norms, regional preferences, and local trends vary by geographic location. Adapting content to regional demographics ensures relevance and resonance with local audiences.

Strategies for Adapting Content

- **Tailored Messaging**: Customize your messaging to reflect the values, aspirations, and concerns of specific demographic segments. Use language and tone that resonates with their interests and priorities.
- **Content Formats**: Choose content formats that align with demographic preferences. For instance, visual content like infographics or videos may appeal more to younger audiences, while detailed whitepapers may attract professionals in specific industries.
- **Channel Selection**: Select channels and platforms where your target demographics are most active. Adapt content distribution strategies to reach audiences effectively on their preferred channels, whether it's social media, blogs, email newsletters, or offline channels.
- **Visual and Cultural Sensitivity**: Consider visual aesthetics and cultural sensitivities when adapting content to diverse demographic groups. Use imagery, colors, and symbols that are appropriate and resonate positively with your audience.
- **Personalization**: Implement personalization strategies based on demographic data to deliver targeted content experiences. Segment your audience and tailor content recommendations, email campaigns, and offers to meet the specific needs and preferences of each demographic segment.

Measurement and Optimization

- **Analytics**: Use analytics tools to track the performance of demographic-targeted content. Measure metrics such as engagement rates, conversion rates, and audience demographics to evaluate effectiveness.
- **Feedback and Iteration**: Gather feedback from your audience through surveys, comments, and social media interactions. Use insights to iterate and optimize content strategies continuously, ensuring relevance and effectiveness.
- **A/B Testing**: Experiment with different content adaptations and formats to identify what resonates best with each demographic segment. Use A/B testing to compare performance and refine content strategies based on data-driven insights.

Adapting content to audience demographics is a strategic approach to enhance engagement, relevance, and impact in content marketing efforts. By understanding the unique characteristics and preferences of your audience segments, you can create personalized, compelling content that connects with your target audience on a deeper level. Continuously refining your content strategies based on demographic insights ensures that your messages resonate effectively and drive desired outcomes in your marketing efforts.

Chapter 3: Crafting Engaging Content

Crafting engaging content is a fundamental aspect of successful content marketing. It involves creating valuable, relevant, and compelling material that resonates with your audience, encourages interaction, and supports your overall marketing goals. In this chapter, we will explore strategies and techniques to effectively craft engaging content that captivates your audience and drives meaningful interactions.

Effective content engagement hinges on several key factors. First and foremost is relevance—ensuring that your content addresses timely topics and aligns with the interests and needs of your audience. Quality is equally crucial; delivering well-researched, informative, and valuable content establishes credibility and fosters trust with your readers. Authenticity plays a vital role as well, as maintaining a genuine voice and tone that reflects your brand identity helps in building a strong connection with your audience.

Visual appeal enhances engagement significantly. Utilizing compelling visuals such as images, infographics, and videos not only captures attention but also aids in conveying complex information effectively. Interactive elements like polls, quizzes, contests, and calls to action are instrumental in fostering audience participation and boosting engagement metrics. Lastly, creating an emotional connection through your content—whether through humor, empathy, or inspiration—can deepen the impact and resonance of your message with your audience.

Crafting engaging content starts with strategic planning and creative ideation. Clearly defining your content objectives—whether it's driving traffic, increasing brand awareness, or generating leads—is essential. Utilizing audience research and insights from personas helps in developing content ideas that are tailored to resonate with your target audience. Keyword research ensures that your content aligns with search intent and is optimized for search engine visibility. Establishing a content calendar ensures consistency and relevance in your content publishing schedule.

Compelling copywriting and visual presentation are crucial elements of crafting engaging content. Structuring your content with clear headings, subheadings, and well-organized paragraphs improves readability and user experience. Crafting engaging headlines that are both informative and enticing helps grab attention and encourage further reading. Incorporating storytelling techniques—such as narratives, anecdotes, or case studies—can captivate your audience and make your content more memorable. High-quality visuals enhance comprehension and appeal, catering to visual learners and enhancing overall content engagement. Integrating multimedia elements like videos, podcasts, and interactive features diversifies content formats and appeals to different audience preferences.

Optimizing content for search engine optimization (SEO) and accessibility is essential for maximizing reach and ensuring inclusivity. Implementing SEO best practices—such as using relevant keywords, optimizing meta descriptions, and adding alt text for images—improves search engine visibility and organic discoverability. Designing content that is mobile-friendly and responsive ensures a seamless user experience across devices, catering to the growing number of mobile users. Enhancing accessibility features—such as incorporating text-to-speech capabilities, providing captions, and ensuring compatibility with screen readers—makes your content accessible to individuals with disabilities, broadening your audience reach and engagement.

Measuring and iterating content performance is crucial for refining strategies and optimizing future content efforts. Tracking analytics metrics—such as traffic sources, engagement rates, bounce rates, and conversion rates—provides valuable insights into content effectiveness and audience behavior. Conducting A/B testing and experimenting with different content variations helps in identifying what resonates best with your audience and refining content strategies accordingly. Analyzing audience feedback through comments, surveys, and social media interactions offers qualitative insights that inform content improvements and optimizations.

Crafting engaging content is an ongoing process that requires continuous refinement and adaptation to evolving audience preferences and market trends. By focusing on creating valuable, relevant, and interactive content, you can build stronger connections with your audience, enhance brand visibility, and achieve your content marketing objectives effectively. In the following chapters, we will delve deeper into specific content types, distribution strategies, and advanced techniques to further elevate your content marketing efforts.

3.1 The Art of Storytelling

Storytelling is a powerful technique in content creation that captivates audiences, fosters emotional connections, and enhances the overall impact of your message. At its core, storytelling involves crafting narratives that engage, inform, and resonate with your audience on a deeper level. In this section, we will explore the principles and strategies behind effective storytelling in content marketing.

Principles of Effective Storytelling

- **Clarity and Structure**: A well-told story has a clear beginning, middle, and end. It unfolds in a structured manner that guides the audience through a cohesive narrative arc, building anticipation and delivering resolution.

- **Relatability**: Stories that resonate with the audience's experiences, emotions, and aspirations are more likely to capture attention and create lasting impressions. Relatable characters and situations make the story more compelling and memorable.
- **Emotional Appeal**: Emotions play a central role in storytelling. By evoking emotions such as empathy, joy, fear, or inspiration, stories can forge deep connections with the audience, making them more engaged and receptive to your message.
- **Authenticity**: Authentic storytelling is genuine and reflective of your brand's values, voice, and personality. It establishes credibility and trust with your audience, fostering stronger relationships over time.
- **Conflict and Resolution**: Every compelling story revolves around conflict—a challenge or obstacle that the protagonist must overcome. The resolution of this conflict provides closure and satisfaction, leaving the audience with a sense of fulfillment.

Strategies for Crafting Compelling Stories

- **Know Your Audience**: Understand the demographics, interests, and preferences of your audience to tailor your story to their expectations and emotional triggers.
- **Identify a Central Theme**: Choose a central theme or message that aligns with your brand values and resonates with your audience's interests or pain points.
- **Create Vivid Characters**: Develop characters—whether fictional or based on real-life experiences—that are relatable, empathetic, and memorable. Characters drive the narrative and connect with your audience on a personal level.

- **Use Descriptive Language and Imagery**: Paint a vivid picture through descriptive language, sensory details, and visual imagery. Engage the audience's imagination to immerse them in the story's world.
- **Maintain Tension and Momentum**: Keep the audience engaged by maintaining suspense, intrigue, or curiosity throughout the storytelling process. Build tension gradually and sustain momentum to sustain interest until the story's resolution.
- **Include a Call to Action**: Conclude your story with a clear call to action that prompts the audience to take the next step—whether it's visiting your website, subscribing to your newsletter, or making a purchase. A compelling call to action capitalizes on the emotional engagement fostered by the story.

Application in Content Marketing

In content marketing, storytelling can be applied across various formats and channels:

- **Blog Posts and Articles**: Use storytelling techniques to craft engaging introductions, illustrate concepts with anecdotes, or share customer success stories.
- **Videos and Podcasts**: Create narrative-driven content that unfolds through storytelling, combining visual or auditory elements to enhance emotional impact.
- **Social Media**: Share micro-stories, behind-the-scenes glimpses, or user-generated content that resonates with your audience's interests and emotions.

- **Case Studies and Testimonials**: Present real-life examples and narratives that demonstrate the effectiveness of your products or services in solving customer challenges.

Mastering the art of storytelling is a powerful skill that enhances content marketing efforts by creating meaningful connections with your audience. By crafting compelling narratives that are clear, relatable, emotionally resonant, and authentic, you can capture attention, inspire action, and achieve your marketing objectives effectively. In the following sections, we will explore additional strategies and techniques to further elevate your content creation and storytelling abilities.

3.2 Writing Compelling Headlines

Writing compelling headlines is essential for capturing the attention of your audience and enticing them to engage with your content. A headline serves as the first impression of your piece, influencing whether readers click through to read more. In this section, we will explore strategies and best practices for crafting headlines that are compelling, engaging, and effective in content marketing.

Key Elements of Compelling Headlines

- **Clarity and Conciseness**: A compelling headline communicates the main idea or benefit of the content concisely. It should be easy to understand at a glance.

- **Relevance**: Headlines should be relevant to the content they introduce, accurately reflecting the topic or main message of the article, blog post, or piece of content.
- **Interest and Intrigue**: Engaging headlines pique curiosity and provoke interest. They create a desire in the reader to learn more or find out what the content has to offer.
- **Actionable Language**: Using actionable words or phrases encourages readers to take immediate interest. Words like "discover," "learn," "unlock," "master," or "explore" can prompt action and engagement.
- **Unique Value Proposition**: Highlighting a unique benefit, insight, or solution offered in the content can make the headline more compelling. It should convey why the reader should invest their time in consuming the content.

Strategies for Crafting Effective Headlines

- **Use Numbers and Lists**: Headlines that include numbers (e.g., "5 Ways to Improve Your Writing Skills") or lists ("Top 10 Tips for SEO Optimization") are attractive because they promise specific information and structure.
- **Pose Questions**: Questions in headlines provoke curiosity and encourage readers to seek answers within the content. For example, "Are You Making These Common Mistakes in Content Marketing?"
- **Create Urgency**: Headlines that create a sense of urgency or convey a timely opportunity can prompt immediate action. Phrases like "Limited Time Offer," "Act Now," or "Don't Miss Out" can be effective.

- **Use Power Words**: Power words are persuasive and emotional words that evoke strong responses. Examples include "ultimate," "effective," "essential," "revolutionary," "proven," "free," and "guaranteed."
- **Tailor to Your Audience**: Consider the preferences, interests, and language of your target audience. Tailor headlines to resonate with their needs and motivations.

Writing Process and Tips

- **Draft Multiple Versions**: Brainstorm several headline ideas before choosing the most compelling one. Experiment with different angles, tones, and structures.
- **Test and Iterate**: A/B testing can help determine which headline resonates best with your audience. Use analytics tools to track click-through rates and engagement metrics.
- **Avoid Clickbait**: While it's important to create compelling headlines, avoid misleading or sensationalist tactics that can disappoint readers and damage your brand's credibility.
- **SEO Considerations**: Incorporate relevant keywords naturally into your headlines to improve search engine visibility and attract organic traffic.
- **Stay Updated**: Stay informed about current trends, news, and industry buzzwords that can enhance the relevance and appeal of your headlines.

Writing compelling headlines is both an art and a science that requires creativity, strategic thinking, and an understanding of your audience. By crafting clear, relevant, and intriguing headlines that convey value and provoke curiosity, you can effectively attract attention, drive traffic, and engage readers with your content. In the next sections, we will delve deeper into additional aspects of creating engaging content, including structuring content for readability, optimizing for SEO, and leveraging multimedia elements.

3.3 Structuring Your Content

Structuring your content effectively is crucial for engaging your audience, enhancing readability, and delivering your message clearly and persuasively. A well-organized structure guides readers through your content, helps them understand key points, and encourages them to stay engaged until the end. In this section, we will explore strategies and best practices for structuring your content to maximize its impact and effectiveness in content marketing.

Importance of Content Structure

- **Clarity and Coherence**: A structured approach ensures that your content is organized logically, with a clear flow of ideas and information. This clarity makes it easier for readers to follow and understand your message.
- **Engagement and Readability**: A well-structured content layout— featuring headings, subheadings, and paragraphs—enhances readability by breaking up text and providing visual cues. This encourages readers to consume the content more comprehensively.
- **Highlighting Key Information**: Structuring allows you to emphasize important points and insights effectively. Strategic use

of formatting (e.g., bold text, bullet points) draws attention to key takeaways, making them more memorable for readers.

- **SEO Optimization**: Organized content improves SEO by making it easier for search engines to crawl and understand your content. Clear headings and relevant keywords contribute to higher visibility in search engine results pages (SERPs).

Best Practices for Structuring Content

- **Introduction**: Start with a compelling introduction that captures attention and outlines what readers can expect from the content. Clearly state the purpose or main idea to set expectations.
- **Headings and Subheadings**: Use descriptive and hierarchical headings to organize your content into sections and sub-sections. Headings not only structure the content but also help readers navigate and find information quickly.
- **Logical Flow**: Arrange content in a logical sequence that guides readers from one point to the next. Use transitions and logical connectors to maintain coherence and flow between paragraphs and sections.
- **Paragraphs and Formatting**: Keep paragraphs concise and focused on a single idea or topic. Use formatting techniques such as bullet points, numbered lists, and bold text to highlight key information and improve readability.
- **Visual Elements**: Incorporate visuals—such as images, infographics, and charts—to complement textual content and enhance understanding. Place visuals strategically to reinforce key points and break up text.

- **Conclusion**: Summarize key takeaways and reinforce the main message in the conclusion. Provide a clear call to action (CTA) or next steps for readers to take after consuming the content.

Writing Process and Tips

- **Outline**: Create an outline before writing to organize your thoughts and determine the structure of your content. Outline main sections, sub-sections, and key points to cover.
- **Draft and Revise**: Write the first draft focusing on content flow and clarity. Revise the structure to improve coherence, remove redundancies, and refine transitions between sections.
- **Peer Review**: Seek feedback from peers or colleagues to evaluate the effectiveness of your content structure. Use their insights to make necessary adjustments and improvements.
- **Test Readability**: Assess the readability of your content by considering factors like sentence length, vocabulary complexity, and overall readability score. Tools like Hemingway Editor or Readable.io can help analyze readability metrics.
- **Optimize for Mobile**: Ensure that your content structure is responsive and mobile-friendly. Test how the content appears and functions on various devices to provide a seamless user experience.

Effective content structure is integral to delivering engaging, readable, and persuasive content that resonates with your audience. By organizing your content logically, emphasizing key information, and enhancing readability through headings, formatting, and visuals, you can effectively communicate your message and achieve your content marketing goals. In the upcoming sections, we will explore additional strategies for optimizing content for SEO, leveraging multimedia elements, and measuring content performance to enhance overall effectiveness.

3.4 Tips for Writing Clear and Concise Content

Writing clear and concise content is essential for effectively communicating your message, engaging your audience, and achieving your content marketing objectives. Clear and concise writing enhances readability, improves comprehension, and ensures that your content delivers value efficiently. In this section, we will explore practical tips and strategies to help you write clear and concise content.

Why Clear and Concise Content Matters

- **Clarity**: Clear content is easy to understand and eliminates ambiguity. It ensures that your audience grasps your message accurately without confusion or misinterpretation.
- **Conciseness**: Concise content gets to the point quickly and efficiently. It respects your audience's time by delivering information succinctly and without unnecessary filler or verbosity.
- **Engagement**: Clear and concise writing holds readers' attention and encourages them to stay engaged with your content. It reduces cognitive load and makes it easier for readers to absorb information.
- **Professionalism**: Writing that is clear and concise reflects positively on your professionalism and expertise. It enhances your credibility and builds trust with your audience.

Tips for Writing Clear and Concise Content

- **Know Your Audience**: Understand the demographics, preferences, and knowledge level of your audience. Tailor your language and complexity of information accordingly to ensure clarity.
- **Plan and Outline**: Before you start writing, outline your main points and structure your content logically. Organize ideas in a sequential flow that makes sense and guides readers through the content smoothly.
- **Use Simple Language**: Choose plain language and avoid jargon, technical terms, or complex vocabulary unless necessary. Aim for clarity by using words that are familiar and easily understood by your audience.
- **Be Direct and Specific**: Get to the point quickly and avoid unnecessary tangents or excessive details. State your main idea or message early in the content and support it with relevant, concise information.
- **Use Short Sentences and Paragraphs**: Break down information into shorter sentences and paragraphs to improve readability. This helps readers digest information more easily and keeps them engaged.
- **Avoid Redundancy and Wordiness**: Eliminate redundant phrases, unnecessary adjectives, and filler words that do not add value to your content. Every word should contribute meaningfully to your message.
- **Use Headings and Subheadings**: Organize content into sections with descriptive headings and subheadings. This helps readers navigate and find information quickly, enhancing overall clarity.
- **Edit and Revise**: Review your content critically to remove any unclear or convoluted sentences. Simplify complex ideas without

oversimplifying critical information. Aim for clarity without sacrificing depth.
- **Get Feedback**: Have peers or colleagues review your content to provide constructive feedback on clarity and readability. Fresh perspectives can identify areas that need improvement.
- **Read Aloud**: Reading your content aloud can help identify awkward phrasing, unclear sentences, or areas where the flow could be improved. This technique can enhance overall clarity and coherence.

Writing clear and concise content is a skill that enhances the effectiveness of your content marketing efforts. By focusing on simplicity, clarity, and directness, you can deliver information effectively, engage your audience, and achieve your communication goals more efficiently. Incorporate these tips into your writing process to create content that is clear, concise, and impactful. In the following sections, we will delve deeper into optimizing content for SEO, incorporating multimedia elements, and measuring content performance to further enhance your content strategy.

3.5 Using Visuals to Enhance Engagement

Visuals are powerful tools in content marketing that enhance engagement, improve comprehension, and make your content more memorable. Integrating compelling visuals—such as images, infographics, videos, and charts—can significantly boost the effectiveness of your content by appealing to both visual learners and those who prefer interactive content formats. In this section, we will explore strategies and best practices for using visuals to enhance engagement in your content.

Benefits of Using Visuals

- **Enhanced Engagement**: Visuals capture attention and encourage interaction with your content. They break up text-heavy sections and provide visual relief, keeping readers engaged and interested.
- **Improved Comprehension**: Complex information can be easier to understand and retain when presented visually. Visuals help illustrate concepts, processes, and data points clearly and intuitively.
- **Increased Memorability**: Visual content is more likely to be remembered compared to text alone. Images and graphics create stronger impressions and help reinforce key messages or ideas.
- **Diverse Content Formats**: Visuals allow you to diversify your content formats and cater to different audience preferences. Whether through videos, infographics, or interactive images, visuals offer versatility in presenting information.

Types of Visuals to Consider

- **Images and Photographs**: Use high-quality images and photographs that align with your content's theme and resonate with your audience. Visual storytelling through images can evoke emotions and enhance narrative impact.
- **Infographics**: Infographics visually represent data, statistics, or processes using charts, graphs, icons, and concise text. They condense complex information into digestible, shareable formats that are ideal for social media and content sharing.
- **Videos**: Video content engages audiences through dynamic visuals, audio narration, and storytelling. Use videos for tutorials,

demonstrations, customer testimonials, or behind-the-scenes insights to connect with your audience on a deeper level.

- **Charts and Graphs**: Visualize numerical data and trends using charts (e.g., bar charts, pie charts) and graphs. Visual representations of data help readers grasp insights quickly and make data-driven decisions.
- **Interactive Visuals**: Incorporate interactive elements such as clickable infographics, interactive maps, or sliders that engage users and encourage exploration. Interactive visuals enhance user experience and increase time spent on your content.

Best Practices for Using Visuals Effectively

- **Relevance**: Choose visuals that are relevant to your content's message and audience interests. Align visuals with the context and tone of your content to maintain consistency.
- **Quality**: Use high-resolution images and professionally designed graphics to ensure visual appeal and clarity. Poor-quality visuals can detract from your content's credibility.
- **Accessibility**: Ensure that visuals are accessible to all users, including those with disabilities. Provide alternative text (alt text) for images, captions for videos, and consider color contrast for readability.
- **Integration with Text**: Integrate visuals strategically with text to complement and enhance the narrative. Use visuals to illustrate key points, provide examples, or break down complex information.
- **Optimization for SEO**: Optimize image filenames, alt text, and descriptions with relevant keywords to improve SEO and increase visibility in search engine results.

Tools and Resources

- **Canva**: A user-friendly tool for creating graphics, infographics, and social media visuals.
- **Adobe Spark**: Create stunning visuals, web pages, and short videos with easy-to-use templates.
- **Pixabay and Unsplash**: Sources for high-quality, free images and photographs.
- **Venngage and Infogram**: Platforms for creating interactive infographics and data visualizations.

Visuals play a crucial role in enhancing engagement, improving comprehension, and making your content more memorable. By incorporating relevant and high-quality visuals—such as images, infographics, videos, and interactive elements—you can effectively communicate your message, captivate your audience, and achieve your content marketing goals. Experiment with different visual formats and integrate them strategically into your content to maximize impact and enhance user experience. In the upcoming sections, we will explore additional strategies for optimizing content for SEO, measuring content performance, and refining your content marketing strategy.

Chapter 4: SEO Fundamentals for Content Writers

Search Engine Optimization (SEO) is a critical component of content writing that enhances visibility, increases organic traffic, and improves search engine rankings. Understanding SEO fundamentals empowers content writers to create content that is not only engaging but also optimized for search engines. In this chapter, we will delve into essential SEO principles, techniques, and best practices that every content writer should know to effectively optimize their content for search engines.

1. Understanding SEO Basics

SEO is the practice of optimizing web content—such as articles, blog posts, and web pages—to rank higher in search engine results pages (SERPs) for relevant keywords and phrases. The primary goals of SEO include increasing visibility, driving organic traffic, and attracting qualified leads or customers to your website.

2. Importance of Keywords

Keywords are fundamental to SEO and serve as the bridge between what users are searching for and the content you provide. Content writers should conduct keyword research to identify relevant keywords and phrases that align with their content topics and target audience. Incorporating keywords naturally and strategically throughout the content helps improve search engine visibility and relevance.

3. On-Page SEO Optimization

On-page SEO focuses on optimizing individual web pages to rank higher and earn more relevant traffic in search engines. Key aspects of on-page SEO include:

- **Title Tags**: Crafting unique, descriptive titles that include primary keywords.
- **Meta Descriptions**: Write concise summaries that entice users to click through to the content.
- **Header Tags**: Using H1, H2, and H3 tags to structure content hierarchically and improve readability.
- **Keyword Optimization**: Strategically placing keywords in headings, paragraphs, and throughout the content.
- **URL Structure**: Creating SEO-friendly URLs that are descriptive and include relevant keywords.

4. Content Quality and Relevance

High-quality, relevant content is essential for SEO success. Content writers should focus on creating valuable, informative, and engaging content that addresses the needs and interests of their target audience. Search engines prioritize content that provides genuine value and satisfies user search intent.

5. Link-Building Strategies

Link building plays a crucial role in SEO by establishing authority and credibility. Content writers can enhance SEO through:

- **Internal Links**: Linking to relevant internal pages within your website to guide users and establish site structure.
- **External Links**: Linking to reputable external sources that provide additional value or context to your content.
- **Backlinks**: Earning backlinks from authoritative websites through guest posting, partnerships, or content promotion.

6. Mobile-Friendliness and User Experience

With the increasing use of mobile devices, optimizing content for mobile-friendliness is vital. Content writers should ensure that web pages are responsive, load quickly, and provide a seamless user experience across all devices. Mobile-friendly websites are favored by search engines and contribute to better SEO performance.

By understanding and implementing SEO best practices—such as keyword optimization, on-page SEO techniques, content quality, link-building strategies, and mobile optimization—content writers can improve visibility, attract organic traffic, and achieve their content marketing objectives effectively. In the following chapters, we will explore advanced SEO strategies, content distribution tactics, and analytics to further enhance your SEO knowledge and content writing skills.

4.1 Introduction to SEO

Search Engine Optimization (SEO) is the process of optimizing digital content to improve its visibility and ranking in search engine results pages (SERPs). It is a fundamental practice in digital marketing aimed at increasing organic (non-paid) traffic to websites by enhancing their relevance and authority in the eyes of search engines like Google, Bing, and Yahoo.

Key Concepts of SEO

- **Visibility and Ranking**: SEO aims to make web pages more visible to users searching for relevant topics or keywords. Higher rankings in search results can lead to increased website traffic and exposure.
- **Search Engine Algorithms**: Search engines use complex algorithms to determine the relevance and ranking of web pages for specific search queries. Understanding these algorithms helps content writers optimize content effectively.
- **User Intent**: SEO focuses on understanding and satisfying user intent—the reason behind a user's search query. Content that aligns with user intent is more likely to rank well and attract engaged visitors.
- **Keywords**: Keywords are phrases or terms that users type into search engines to find information. Incorporating relevant keywords strategically in content helps search engines understand the topic and context of the content.
- **On-Page and Off-Page Optimization**: On-page SEO involves optimizing individual web pages with elements such as keywords, meta tags, and content structure. Off-page SEO includes activities

like link building and social media promotion that enhance a website's authority and reputation.

Benefits of SEO for Content Writers

- **Increased Traffic**: Optimizing content for SEO can attract more organic traffic to your website, reducing reliance on paid advertising.
- **Improved Visibility**: Higher search engine rankings increase your content's visibility to a broader audience, potentially leading to more exposure and opportunities.
- **Enhanced User Experience**: SEO encourages content writers to create valuable, user-friendly content that meets the needs of their target audience, improving overall user experience.
- **Measurable Results**: SEO efforts can be tracked and measured using analytics tools to evaluate the effectiveness of strategies and adjust tactics as needed.

Understanding the basics of SEO is essential for content writers aiming to create content that not only resonates with their audience but also ranks well in search engine results. By implementing SEO best practices—such as keyword research, on-page optimization, and user-focused content creation—content writers can enhance visibility, attract organic traffic, and achieve their content marketing goals effectively. In the following sections, we will delve deeper into specific SEO strategies, techniques, and tools to further optimize your content and maximize its impact.

4.2 Keyword Research and Selection

Keyword research is a foundational aspect of SEO that involves identifying the terms and phrases users enter into search engines when looking for information related to your content. Choosing the right keywords and integrating them strategically into your content can significantly impact your website's visibility and traffic. In this section, we will explore the importance of keyword research, methods for conducting it effectively, and best practices for selecting keywords.

Importance of Keyword Research

- **Understanding User Intent**: Keyword research helps content writers understand what their target audience is searching for and their underlying intent. By aligning content with relevant keywords, writers can create content that meets user needs and expectations.
- **Improving Search Engine Rankings**: Incorporating targeted keywords into your content signals to search engines that your content is relevant to specific search queries. This can lead to higher rankings in SERPs, increasing visibility and attracting organic traffic.
- **Content Optimization**: Keyword research guides content optimization efforts by identifying high-traffic keywords and related topics. Writers can structure their content around these keywords to enhance relevance and improve SEO performance.
- **Competitive Analysis**: Analyzing competitor keywords provides insights into industry trends, content gaps, and opportunities to differentiate your content. It helps identify keywords that

competitors are ranking for and areas where you can compete effectively.

Methods for Conducting Keyword Research

- **Use Keyword Research Tools**: Utilize tools such as Google Keyword Planner, SEMrush, Ahrefs, or Moz Keyword Explorer to discover relevant keywords, search volumes, and competition levels. These tools provide data-driven insights to inform your keyword strategy.
- **Brainstorming and Mind Mapping**: Start by brainstorming topics related to your content and generate a list of potential keywords. Use mind-mapping techniques to visualize keyword relationships and expand your keyword pool.
- **Analyzing Search Queries**: Review search engine autocomplete suggestions, related search queries, and "People also ask" sections to identify long-tail keywords and variations that users commonly search for.
- **Competitor Analysis**: Analyze competitor websites and content to identify keywords they are ranking for. Identify gaps in their keyword strategy that you can capitalize on to attract relevant traffic.

Best Practices for Selecting Keywords

- **Relevance and Specificity**: Choose keywords that are relevant to your content and specific to your target audience's interests. Long-tail keywords (phrases with three or more words) often have less competition and more focused intent.

- **Search Volume and Competition**: Balance between high search volume keywords and competition levels. Targeting low-competition keywords can be advantageous for newer websites to gain initial traction.
- **Intent Alignment**: Consider the search intent behind keywords—whether informational, navigational, transactional, or commercial investigation. Tailor your content to match the intent to attract qualified traffic.
- **Long-Term Strategy**: Develop a mix of short-term and long-term keyword strategies. Short-term keywords may focus on immediate traffic gains, while long-term keywords aim for sustained visibility and authority.
- **Monitor and Adjust**: Regularly monitor keyword performance using analytics tools. Adjust your keyword strategy based on performance metrics such as click-through rates, bounce rates, and conversions to optimize content effectiveness.

Effective keyword research and selection are essential for maximizing the impact of your content marketing efforts. By understanding user intent, utilizing keyword research tools, analyzing competitors, and selecting relevant keywords, content writers can optimize their content for improved search engine rankings, increased visibility, and enhanced user engagement. In the next chapter, we will explore on-page SEO techniques, including how to integrate selected keywords into content effectively to enhance SEO performance.

4.3 On-Page SEO Techniques

On-page SEO (Search Engine Optimization) refers to optimizing individual web pages to rank higher and earn more relevant traffic in search engines. It involves various techniques and best practices aimed at improving the content, structure, and HTML source code of a page. In this section, we will explore essential on-page SEO techniques that content writers can implement to enhance their content's visibility and search engine rankings.

Key On-Page SEO Elements

Keyword Optimization:

- **Keyword Placement**: Strategically place primary and related keywords in key areas such as the title tag, meta description, headings (H1, H2, H3 tags), and throughout the content.
- **Keyword Density**: Maintain a natural keyword density (around 1-2%) to avoid keyword stuffing, which can negatively impact readability and SEO.

Content Quality:

- **High-Quality Content**: Create informative, valuable, and relevant content that addresses the search intent of your target audience.
- **Readability**: Structure content with short paragraphs, bullet points, and headings to enhance readability and user experience.

Meta Tags:

- **Title Tag**: Craft unique, compelling title tags (around 60 characters) that include primary keywords and accurately describe the content of the page.
- **Meta Description**: Write concise meta descriptions (around 160 characters) that summarize the page content and encourage clicks from search engine users.

Header Tags:

- **H1 Tag**: Use a single H1 tag for the main title or headline of the page, incorporating primary keywords where appropriate.
- **H2-H6 Tags**: Organize content with hierarchical heading tags (H2 to H6) to structure information logically and improve readability.

URL Structure:

- **SEO-Friendly URLs**: Create clean, descriptive URLs that include relevant keywords and accurately reflect the content of the page.
- **Avoid Complex URLs**: Minimize the use of parameters, session IDs, and unnecessary characters in URLs to enhance readability and SEO.

Internal Linking:

- **Link to Relevant Pages**: Use internal links to connect related content within your website. This helps search engines crawl and index pages more effectively.
- **Anchor Text**: Use descriptive anchor text that includes keywords to provide context about the linked content.

Image Optimization:

- **Alt Text**: Optimize image alt attributes with descriptive text that includes relevant keywords. Alt text helps search engines understand the content of images.
- **File Names**: Rename image files using descriptive keywords before uploading them to improve SEO and accessibility.

Page Speed and Mobile Optimization:

- **Page Load Speed**: Ensure fast loading times by optimizing images, leveraging browser caching, and minimizing unnecessary scripts.
- **Mobile-Friendly Design**: Use responsive web design to ensure that your pages are mobile-friendly and provide a seamless user experience across devices.

Best Practices for On-Page SEO

- **Regularly Update Content**: Keep content fresh and relevant to maintain search engine rankings and engage your audience.
- **Monitor Performance**: Use analytics tools to track on-page SEO metrics such as organic traffic, bounce rates, and average session duration.
- **Optimize for User Experience**: Prioritize user experience by focusing on content quality, readability, and ease of navigation.
- **Follow SEO Guidelines**: Stay updated with SEO trends, algorithm changes, and best practices to adapt your strategies accordingly.

Implementing effective on-page SEO techniques is crucial for maximizing the visibility and performance of your web pages in search engine results. By optimizing content with targeted keywords, improving usability and accessibility, and adhering to SEO best practices, content writers can enhance their website's SEO foundation and attract organic traffic effectively. In the next chapter, we will explore off-page SEO strategies, including link-building techniques and content promotion, to further strengthen your SEO efforts.

4.4 The Importance of Meta Descriptions and Tags

Meta descriptions and Meta tags are critical elements of on-page SEO that significantly influence a web page's visibility and performance in search engine results pages (SERPs).

Meta Descriptions:

Meta descriptions serve as concise summaries of web page content. They appear below the title tag in search results and play a crucial role in attracting users to click through to your website. While Meta descriptions themselves do not directly impact rankings, they contribute to click-through rates (CTR). A well-crafted Meta description that accurately reflects the content and includes relevant keywords can entice users to choose your link over others. Higher CTRs send positive signals to search engines, potentially leading to improved rankings over time.

When writing Meta descriptions, it's essential to keep them concise (around 150-160 characters) to ensure they are fully visible in SERPs. They should provide a clear and compelling overview of what users can expect from visiting the page, encouraging them to click through. Including a call to action (CTA) when appropriate can further enhance their effectiveness.

Meta Tags:

Meta tags encompass various HTML elements that provide information about a web page to search engines and website visitors.

- **Title Tag**: Perhaps the most critical Meta tag, the title tag defines the title of the web page and appears as the clickable headline in search results. It directly influences CTRs and helps search engines understand the topic and relevance of the content. Including primary keywords near the beginning of the title tag and keeping it under 60 characters ensures optimal visibility and relevance in SERPs.

- **Meta Keywords**: Previously used to specify keywords relevant to the content, Meta keywords are no longer considered a ranking factor by major search engines due to misuse and spamming practices. However, incorporating relevant keywords naturally within your content remains beneficial for SEO purposes.
- **Meta Robots**: This Meta tag provides instructions to search engine crawlers on how to index and display web page content. Options include "index" (allow indexing), "noindex" (prevent indexing), "follow" (allow following links), and "nofollow" (prevent following links). Proper use of Meta robot tags ensures that search engines crawl and index web pages correctly, preventing issues such as duplicate content penalties.

In conclusion, optimizing Meta descriptions and tags is essential for maximizing your web page's visibility, attracting organic traffic, and enhancing user engagement. By crafting compelling Meta descriptions that accurately represent your content and optimizing title tags and Meta robot directives strategically, content writers can improve their SEO efforts and provide valuable information to users in search engine results. These elements contribute to a stronger SEO foundation and better overall performance in organic search rankings.

4.5 Utilizing SEO Tools and Analytics

Effective utilization of SEO tools and analytics is essential for optimizing content, measuring performance, and making informed decisions to enhance search engine visibility and user engagement. In this section, we will explore the key aspects of using SEO tools and analytics effectively.

SEO Tools for Keyword Research and Analysis

SEO tools play a crucial role in identifying relevant keywords, analyzing competitors, and tracking keyword performance. Popular tools include:

- **Google Keyword Planner**: Helps discover new keywords, estimate search volume, and understand keyword competition.
- **SEMrush**: Provides comprehensive keyword research, competitor analysis, and SEO audit tools.
- **Ahrefs**: Offers insights into organic search traffic, backlinks analysis, and keyword research.
- **Moz Keyword Explorer**: Helps find keywords, assess their difficulty, and track rankings over time.

Website Audit and Performance Tools

These tools assess website health, identify technical SEO issues, and improve overall performance:

- **Google Search Console**: Provides insights into how Google views your site, monitors website performance, and identifies indexing issues.
- **SEMrush Site Audit**: Offers a detailed analysis of on-page SEO issues, site performance, and recommendations for improvement.
- **Ahrefs Site Audit**: Checks for SEO issues, and broken links, and provides suggestions for optimizing site structure.

Analytics Tools for Performance Measurement

Analytics tools track and measure website performance metrics, user behavior, and SEO effectiveness:

- **Google Analytics**: Tracks website traffic, user behavior, and conversion rates, and provides insights into audience demographics.
- **SEMrush Analytics**: Offers traffic analytics, keyword rankings, backlink analysis, and competitive insights.
- **Moz Pro Analytics**: Tracks keyword rankings, monitors site performance, and provides actionable insights for SEO improvement.

Benefits of Using SEO Tools and Analytics

- **Data-Driven Decisions**: Access to comprehensive data helps make informed decisions regarding content optimization, keyword targeting, and overall SEO strategy.
- **Competitive Analysis**: Analyzing competitor strategies helps identify opportunities and gaps to improve your SEO efforts.
- **Performance Monitoring**: Track key metrics such as organic traffic, keyword rankings, and engagement metrics to measure SEO success and identify areas for improvement.
- **Technical SEO Insights**: Identify and fix technical issues that may affect website performance and search engine visibility.

Implementing Insights from SEO Tools

- **Keyword Optimization**: Use keyword research insights to optimize content with relevant keywords and improve search engine rankings.
- **Content Strategy**: Analyze top-performing content and user engagement metrics to refine content strategy and create more targeted, valuable content.
- **Technical Fixes**: Address technical SEO issues identified by tools to enhance website performance and user experience.

Utilizing SEO tools and analytics effectively is crucial for optimizing content, improving search engine visibility, and achieving long-term SEO success. By leveraging insights from keyword research tools, website audits, and analytics platforms, content writers and marketers can refine their SEO strategies, attract more organic traffic, and enhance user engagement. Continuous monitoring and adjustment based on data-driven insights are key to maintaining and improving SEO performance over time.

Chapter 5: Writing for Different Platforms

Writing for different platforms requires understanding the unique characteristics, audience expectations, and best practices of each medium. Whether creating content for websites, blogs, social media, or other digital channels, adapting your writing style and approach is essential to effectively engage your audience and achieve your content marketing goals.

Website Content:

Writing for websites involves creating informative, structured, and user-friendly content that educates and informs visitors. Focus on clear communication, concise language, and incorporating relevant keywords for SEO. Organize content logically with headers, subheadings, and bullet points to improve readability and navigation. Ensure the content aligns with the website's overall branding and objectives.

Blog Posts:

Blog writing aims to provide valuable, engaging, and shareable content that attracts readers and encourages interaction. Start with compelling headlines to capture attention and include relevant keywords for SEO. Structure blog posts with an introduction, main body, and conclusion. Incorporate visuals, such as images or infographics, to enhance readability and illustrate key points. Encourage reader engagement through comments, social sharing buttons, and calls to action.

Social Media Content:

Writing for social media requires concise, attention-grabbing, and engaging content tailored to each platform's audience and format. Use hashtags effectively on platforms like Twitter and Instagram to increase visibility. Craft compelling captions for posts on Facebook and LinkedIn that encourage likes, comments, and shares. Adapt content length and tone to fit the platform's style and audience preferences while maintaining brand voice and authenticity.

Email Marketing Campaigns:

Email writing involves creating personalized, relevant, and compelling content to engage subscribers and drive action. Start with a clear and captivating subject line to increase open rates. Segment your audience to deliver targeted content that addresses their specific needs or interests. Use a conversational tone, concise language, and compelling call to action (CTA) to encourage click-throughs and conversions. Monitor performance metrics, such as open rates and click-through rates, to refine your email content strategy.

Content Distribution Channels:

Tailor your writing style and content format to suit various distribution channels, such as newsletters, ebooks, whitepapers, and podcasts. Focus on delivering valuable insights, solving audience pain points, and showcasing your expertise. Adapt content length, structure, and visual elements to enhance engagement and readability across different formats. Leverage analytics to measure content performance and optimize distribution strategies for maximum impact.

Cross-Platform Consistency:

Maintain consistency in brand voice, messaging, and quality across all platforms to reinforce brand identity and build trust with your audience. Adapt content strategies based on platform-specific best practices and audience behavior insights. Continuously monitor and analyze performance metrics to refine your content approach and achieve your marketing objectives effectively.

In conclusion, mastering the art of writing for different platforms involves adapting your content strategy, style, and approach to meet the unique demands and expectations of each medium. By understanding audience preferences, leveraging platform-specific features, and optimizing content for SEO and engagement, content creators can effectively reach and resonate with their target audience across diverse digital channels.

5.1 Website Content Writing

Writing content for websites requires a strategic approach to engage visitors, convey information effectively, and achieve business objectives. Website content serves as a crucial touchpoint for potential customers, conveying your brand's message, values, and offerings. Here are key considerations for effective website content writing:

1. Audience Understanding:

Tailor content to address the needs, preferences, and expectations of your target audience. Understand their pain points, interests, and motivations to create relevant and compelling content.

2. Clear Communication:

Use clear and concise language to communicate your message. Avoid jargon and technical terms that may confuse or alienate visitors. Ensure information is easy to understand and navigate.

3. SEO Integration:

Incorporate relevant keywords naturally throughout your content to improve search engine visibility. Optimize meta tags, headers, and image alt text to enhance SEO performance and attract organic traffic.

4. Structure and Navigation:

Organize content with a logical structure using headings, subheadings, and bullet points. Guide visitors through the content hierarchy to facilitate easy navigation and access to information.

5. Brand Consistency:

Maintain consistency with your brand voice, tone, and messaging across all website pages. Reinforce brand identity through cohesive content that reflects your values and resonates with your audience.

6. Call to Action (CTA):

Include clear and compelling calls to action (CTAs) throughout your website content to encourage visitors to take desired actions, such as making a purchase, signing up for a newsletter, or contacting your business.

7. Visual Elements:

Enhance readability and engagement with visual elements such as images, videos, infographics, and charts. Use visuals strategically to illustrate key points, break up text, and improve overall user experience.

8. Accessibility and Mobile Optimization:

Ensure your website content is accessible to all users, including those with disabilities. Use alt text for images, readable fonts, and responsive design to optimize for mobile devices and improve usability.

9. Regular Updates:

Keep website content fresh and relevant by updating information, addressing new developments, and incorporating feedback from users. Regular updates demonstrate your commitment to providing valuable and up-to-date content.

10. Analytics and Optimization:

Monitor website analytics to track visitor behavior, engagement metrics, and conversion rates. Use data insights to optimize content performance, identify areas for improvement, and refine your content strategy over time.

Effective website content writing combines creativity with strategic planning to engage visitors, enhance user experience, and achieve business objectives. By focusing on audience needs, optimizing for search engines, maintaining brand consistency, and leveraging analytics, content writers can create compelling and impactful content that drives traffic, enhances user engagement, and supports overall digital marketing efforts.

5.2 Blogging Best Practices

Blogging is a powerful tool for businesses and individuals alike to share valuable information, engage with audiences, and improve search engine visibility. To maximize the effectiveness of your blog and attract readers, consider the following best practices:

1. **Define Your Audience:**

Identify your target audience and understand their interests, preferences, and challenges. Tailor your blog content to address their needs and provide valuable insights.

2. **Compelling Headlines:**

Craft attention-grabbing headlines that spark curiosity and encourage readers to click. Include relevant keywords to improve search engine rankings and attract organic traffic.

3. **Informative and Valuable Content:**

Provide informative, well-researched, and valuable content that offers solutions to readers' problems or answers their questions. Position yourself as a credible source of information in your industry.

4. **Consistent Posting Schedule:**

Maintain a consistent posting schedule to keep readers engaged and establish trust. Whether it's weekly, bi-weekly, or monthly, set realistic goals and stick to your publishing schedule.

5. Engaging Writing Style:

Write in a conversational tone that resonates with your audience. Keep paragraphs short, use subheadings, and incorporate bullet points to improve readability and highlight key information.

6. SEO Optimization:

Optimize your blog posts for search engines by including relevant keywords naturally throughout the content. Use headings (H1, H2, etc.), meta descriptions, and alt text for images to enhance SEO performance.

7. Visual Content:

Include visuals such as images, infographics, and videos to complement your written content. Visuals not only enhance reader engagement but also break up text and make your blog posts more appealing.

8. Encourage Interaction:

Foster engagement by encouraging readers to leave comments, share their thoughts, and ask questions. Respond to comments promptly to build a sense of community around your blog.

9. Promote Across Channels:

Promote your blog posts across social media platforms, email newsletters, and other relevant channels to reach a wider audience. Use compelling snippets and visuals to drive traffic back to your blog.

10. Measure and Analyze Performance:

Use analytics tools such as Google Analytics or platform-specific insights to track metrics like page views, bounce rates, and social shares. Analyze performance data to understand what resonates with your audience and adjust your content strategy accordingly.

11. Guest Blogging and Collaboration:

Explore opportunities for guest blogging on reputable sites within your industry. Collaborate with influencers or other bloggers to expand your reach and attract new readers to your blog.

12. Stay Updated and Evolve:

Stay informed about industry trends, changes in search engine algorithms, and evolving reader preferences. Adapt your blogging strategy to incorporate new ideas, formats, and technologies to stay relevant.

By following these blogging best practices, you can create compelling, informative, and engaging content that resonates with your audience, improves search engine rankings, and drives traffic to your blog. Consistency, quality, and an audience-centric approach are key to building a successful and impactful blog presence.

5.3 Social Media Content Strategies

Social media platforms offer powerful avenues to connect with audiences, build brand awareness, and drive engagement. Crafting effective social media content requires understanding platform dynamics, audience preferences, and strategic planning. Here are key strategies to enhance your social media content:

1. **Platform-Specific Content:**

Tailor your content to fit the characteristics and audience behavior of each social media platform (e.g., Facebook, Instagram, Twitter, LinkedIn). Customize content formats, tone, and visuals to resonate with platform users.

2. **Clear Objectives and Messaging:**

Define clear objectives for your social media content, whether it's increasing brand awareness, driving traffic to your website, or promoting a product/service. Align your messaging with these objectives to guide content creation.

3. Consistent Brand Voice:

Maintain a consistent brand voice and tone across all social media channels. Establish a personality that reflects your brand values and resonates with your target audience.

4. Engaging Visuals and Multimedia:

Use high-quality images, videos, infographics, and GIFs to capture attention and convey messages effectively. Visual content tends to perform better and can increase engagement on social media.

5. Compelling Headlines and Captions:

Craft compelling headlines, captions, and descriptions that encourage users to engage with your content. Use relevant hashtags to increase visibility and reach a wider audience.

6. Interactive Content Formats:

Encourage interaction and participation through polls, quizzes, contests, and live videos. Interactive content fosters engagement and strengthens relationships with your audience.

7. Timing and Frequency:

Schedule posts at optimal times when your target audience is most active on each platform. Experiment with posting frequency to maintain visibility without overwhelming your audience.

8. Respond and Engage:

Monitor comments, messages, and mentions on your social media profiles. Respond promptly to inquiries, acknowledge feedback, and engage in conversations to build relationships and foster community.

9. User-Generated Content (UGC):

Encourage followers to create and share content related to your brand or products. UGC can enhance authenticity, credibility, and engagement while showcasing satisfied customers.

10. Analytics and Optimization:

Use analytics tools provided by social media platforms (e.g., Facebook Insights, Instagram Insights) to track performance metrics. Analyze data such as reach, engagement rate, click-throughs, and conversions to refine your content strategy.

11. Paid Advertising Strategies:

Consider using paid social media advertising (e.g., Facebook Ads, LinkedIn Ads) to amplify your reach, target specific audiences, and achieve business objectives such as lead generation or sales.

12. Stay Updated and Experiment:

Stay informed about trends, algorithm changes, and new features on social media platforms. Experiment with different content formats, strategies, and campaigns to identify what resonates best with your audience.

Implementing these social media content strategies can help you create compelling, engaging, and impactful content that resonates with your audience, strengthens brand presence, and drives meaningful interactions on social platforms. Adapt your approach based on platform insights and audience feedback to optimize performance and achieve your marketing goals effectively.

5.4 Email Marketing Content

Email marketing remains a powerful tool for businesses to connect with their audience, nurture leads, and drive conversions. Crafting effective email marketing content involves strategic planning, compelling messaging, and engaging visuals to encourage recipients to take action. Here are key strategies and considerations for creating successful email marketing campaigns:

1. Define Campaign Goals:

Clearly define the objectives of your email marketing campaign, whether it's promoting a product launch, driving traffic to your website, or nurturing leads through a sales funnel. Align your content with these goals to guide your messaging.

2. Audience Segmentation:

Segment your email list based on demographics, behaviors, purchase history, or engagement levels. Tailor your content to address the specific needs, interests, and preferences of each segment to improve relevance and engagement.

3. Personalization and Customization:

Personalize email content by addressing recipients by their name and dynamically inserting relevant information based on their interactions or preferences. Use personalized recommendations, offers, or content suggestions to enhance engagement.

4. Compelling Subject Lines:

Craft attention-grabbing subject lines that pique curiosity and encourage recipients to open your emails. Avoid spammy or misleading subject lines and accurately reflect the content inside.

5. Clear and Concise Messaging:

Use clear and concise language to convey your message effectively. Keep paragraphs short, use bullet points or numbered lists for readability, and highlight key information to make it easily scannable.

6. Visual Appeal:

Incorporate visually appealing elements such as images, graphics, or videos to enhance the overall look and feel of your emails. Use visuals strategically to support your message and encourage engagement.

7. Call to Action (CTA):

Include a clear and compelling call to action (CTA) in your email content that prompts recipients to take the desired action, such as making a purchase, signing up for an event, or downloading a resource. Use actionable language and place CTAs prominently within your email.

8. Mobile Optimization:

Optimize your email content for mobile devices to ensure readability and functionality on smartphones and tablets. Use responsive design, single-column layouts, and appropriately sized fonts to enhance user experience.

9. A/B Testing:

Experiment with different elements of your email campaigns, such as subject lines, CTAs, visuals, or send times, through A/B testing. Analyze results to identify which variations perform best and optimize future campaigns based on insights.

10. Compliance and Legal Considerations:

Ensure your email marketing campaigns comply with data protection regulations (e.g., GDPR, CAN-SPAM Act). Obtain consent from recipients to send marketing emails, provide an option to unsubscribe, and include your company's physical address.

11. Measure Performance and Iteration:

Track key performance metrics such as open rates, click-through rates (CTR), conversion rates, and unsubscribe rates. Use email analytics tools to gain insights into campaign effectiveness and make data-driven decisions for future optimizations.

12. Nurture Relationships:

Focus on building long-term relationships with your audience through consistent, valuable, and relevant email content. Provide useful information, educational resources, and exclusive offers to keep subscribers engaged and loyal.

By implementing these strategies and best practices, you can create compelling email marketing content that resonates with your audience, drives engagement, and supports your business objectives effectively. Continuously monitor performance metrics, adapt your approach based on insights, and refine your email marketing strategy to achieve sustainable growth and success.

5.5 Writing for E-commerce Platforms

Writing effectively for e-commerce platforms involves creating persuasive, informative, and engaging content that drives sales, enhances user experience, and builds brand loyalty. Whether you're writing product descriptions, category pages, promotional content, or customer communications, here are essential strategies and considerations for e-commerce content:

1. Product Descriptions:

Craft detailed and compelling product descriptions that highlight key features, benefits, and unique selling points. Use descriptive language to evoke imagery and help potential customers visualize using the product. Include technical specifications, sizes, materials, and care instructions where applicable.

2. SEO Optimization:

Optimize product descriptions and category pages with relevant keywords to improve search engine rankings and attract organic traffic.

Use keyword research to identify high-traffic keywords and incorporate them naturally into your content.

3.   Clear and Concise Language:

Use clear, straightforward language to communicate product information effectively. Avoid jargon or overly technical terms that may confuse or deter potential buyers. Focus on clarity and simplicity while maintaining professionalism.

4.   Visual Content Integration:

Include high-quality images or videos alongside product descriptions to showcase features, demonstrate functionality, and provide a visual representation of the product. Visual content enhances the shopping experience and encourages purchase decisions.

5.   Benefits-Oriented Approach:

Highlight the benefits and value proposition of each product. Address customer pain points and emphasize how the product solves their problems or fulfills their needs. Focus on the benefits rather than just listing features.

6. Customer Reviews and Testimonials:

Incorporate customer reviews, testimonials, and ratings into product pages to build trust and credibility. Positive reviews serve as social proof and influence purchasing decisions. Respond to customer feedback to demonstrate responsiveness and commitment to customer satisfaction.

7. Promotions and Offers:

Write persuasive promotional content for sales, discounts, or special offers. Communicate the promotion's terms, duration, and benefits to encourage immediate action from potential buyers. Use urgency and scarcity tactics where appropriate.

8. Cross-Selling and Upselling Opportunities:

Recommend related products, accessories, or complementary items to encourage cross-selling and upselling. Use suggestive language and product bundles to increase average order value and enhance the shopping experience.

9. User-Friendly Navigation and Information Architecture:

Ensure product categories, filters, and navigation menus are intuitive and user-friendly. Organize product listings logically and provide easy access to detailed product information, sizing charts, shipping options, and return policies.

10. Mobile Optimization:

Optimize e-commerce content for mobile devices to accommodate users who shop on smartphones and tablets. Use responsive design, fast loading times, and mobile-friendly layouts to enhance usability and facilitate seamless browsing and checkout.

11. Storytelling and Brand Narrative:

Incorporate brand storytelling into product descriptions and category pages to create an emotional connection with customers. Share the brand's values, mission, and unique story to differentiate it from competitors and resonate with your target audience.

12. Continuous Improvement and Testing:

Monitor e-commerce analytics and performance metrics to track conversion rates, average order value, bounce rates, and customer engagement. Conduct A/B testing of product descriptions, visuals, and promotional strategies to optimize content effectiveness and drive sales.

By leveraging these strategies and best practices, e-commerce businesses can create compelling, persuasive, and informative content that enhances the shopping experience, boosts conversions, and fosters customer loyalty. Tailor your approach to meet the specific needs of your target audience while optimizing for search engines and enhancing overall user satisfaction on your e-commerce platform.

Chapter 6: Advanced Content Strategies

Advanced content strategies are pivotal for businesses aiming to elevate their digital presence, engage audiences effectively, and achieve sustained growth. These strategies go beyond basic content creation and incorporate sophisticated approaches to maximize impact and drive meaningful results. Here's an exploration of key advanced content strategies:

1. **Content Personalization:**

Implement dynamic content personalization techniques based on user behavior, preferences, and demographics. Tailor content recommendations, product suggestions, and messaging to individual user profiles to enhance relevance and engagement.

2. **Interactive Content Experiences:**

Create interactive content such as quizzes, polls, calculators, and assessments to actively engage audiences. Interactive experiences foster two-way communication, increase time spent on your site, and generate valuable user data for personalized marketing efforts.

3. **AI-Powered Content Insights:**

Utilize artificial intelligence (AI) tools and algorithms to analyze content performance, predict trends, and optimize strategies. AI can automate content recommendations, personalize user experiences, and enhance content relevance based on real-time data insights.

4. Data-Driven Decision Making:

Leverage data analytics and advanced metrics to inform content strategies and optimizations. Track key performance indicators (KPIs) such as engagement rates, conversion rates, and customer lifetime value (CLV) to refine content tactics and drive ROI.

5. Omnichannel Content Integration:

Develop cohesive content strategies that span multiple channels and touchpoints, ensuring consistent messaging and brand voice across platforms. Integrate content seamlessly across the website, social media, email marketing, and offline channels to provide a unified brand experience.

6. Long-Form and Pillar Content:

Invest in creating comprehensive, in-depth content pieces such as pillar pages, whitepapers, and eBooks that serve as authoritative resources in your industry. Long-form content enhances SEO, establishes thought leadership, and attracts high-quality organic traffic.

7. Content Distribution and Amplification:

Implement strategic content distribution tactics to maximize reach and visibility. Utilize paid promotions, influencer partnerships, guest blogging, and PR campaigns to amplify content exposure and extend your audience reach.

8. Agile Content Iteration:

Adopt agile methodologies to iterate and optimize content based on real-time feedback and performance data. Test variations of headlines, visuals, and CTAs to continually improve content effectiveness and responsiveness to audience preferences.

9. Voice Search Optimization:

Optimize content for voice search queries by incorporating natural language and long-tail keywords. Develop FAQs, structured data markup, and conversational content formats to align with the growing adoption of voice-enabled devices and assistants.

10. Sustainability and Ethical Content Practices:

Embrace sustainable content practices that prioritize authenticity, transparency, and ethical considerations. Develop content that reflects corporate social responsibility (CSR) initiatives, environmental stewardship, and community engagement to resonate with socially conscious audiences.

11. Content Localization and Global Expansion:

Customize content for diverse global markets by adapting language, cultural nuances, and regional preferences. Implement localization strategies to enhance brand relevance and accessibility in international markets while maintaining brand integrity.

12. Continuous Learning and Adaptation:

Stay abreast of emerging trends, technological advancements, and shifts in consumer behavior. Foster a culture of continuous learning and adaptation to innovate content strategies and maintain competitive advantage in dynamic digital landscapes.

By embracing these advanced content strategies, businesses can differentiate themselves, build stronger connections with audiences, and drive sustainable growth. Incorporate these tactics into your content planning and execution to stay ahead of the curve, achieve marketing objectives, and deliver exceptional value to your target audience.

6.1 Creating Evergreen Content

Evergreen content is the cornerstone of a sustainable content marketing strategy, designed to provide lasting value and relevance to your audience over time. Unlike timely or trend-based content, which can quickly become obsolete, evergreen content remains valuable and useful long after its initial publication.

Focus on Evergreen Topics:

Choose topics that address fundamental questions, challenges, or interests within your industry. Examples include comprehensive guides, "how-to" tutorials, or in-depth explanations of core concepts that are unlikely to change significantly.

Comprehensive and In-Depth Coverage:

Provide thorough and detailed information that covers all aspects of the topic. Anticipate common questions and concerns your audience may have, and include practical examples, case studies, statistics, and actionable advice to enhance understanding and utility.

Timeless Value and Utility:

Ensure the content offers lasting value and utility to your audience. Avoid references to specific dates, events, or trends that may quickly become outdated. Instead, focus on principles, strategies, and best practices that remain relevant regardless of time or season.

Search Engine Optimization (SEO):

Optimize evergreen content for relevant keywords and search queries to attract organic traffic over the long term. Conduct thorough keyword research to identify high-volume, low-competition keywords, and integrate them naturally throughout the content.

Update and Maintain Content:

Periodically review and update evergreen content to ensure accuracy, relevance, and freshness. Update statistics, refresh examples, and incorporate new insights or developments to maintain its value and authority as industry standards evolve.

Timeless Formatting and Structure:

Use a clear and organized structure with headings, subheadings, and well-organized paragraphs to improve readability and navigation. Make the content easy to scan and digest for readers seeking specific information or solutions.

Evergreen Visuals and Multimedia:

Include relevant visuals such as infographics, diagrams, or videos that enhance and complement the content. Visual elements should aim to provide additional clarity and understanding without relying on timely or fleeting information.

Promote Evergreen Content Strategically:

Develop a promotion strategy to consistently drive traffic to your evergreen content. Share it across social media platforms, feature it in email newsletters, and incorporate it into relevant blog posts or related content to maximize visibility and reach.

Monitor Performance and Engagement:

Use analytics tools to track the performance of your evergreen content over time. Monitor metrics such as traffic, engagement, time on page, and conversion rates to assess its effectiveness and identify opportunities for improvement or further optimization.

Repurpose and Expand Evergreen Content:

Repurpose successful evergreen content into different formats such as eBooks, podcasts, webinars, or downloadable guides to reach new audiences and reinforce key messages. Expand on popular topics with additional insights or case studies to further enrich the content's value and appeal.

Creating evergreen content requires strategic planning, thorough research, and ongoing optimization to ensure its continued relevance and effectiveness. By focusing on timeless topics, providing comprehensive value, optimizing for SEO, and maintaining content freshness, businesses can create valuable assets that drive long-term engagement, traffic, and conversions.

6.2 Content Repurposing Techniques

Content repurposing involves transforming existing content into different formats or mediums to reach new audiences, extend its lifespan, and maximize its value. By repurposing content, businesses can leverage existing assets to enhance visibility, engagement, and ROI. Here are effective techniques for content repurposing:

1. Blog Posts into Social Media Posts:

Convert blog posts into bite-sized social media updates, infographics, or carousel posts. Highlight key points, quotes, or statistics from the original content to capture attention and drive traffic back to the blog.

2. Webinars into Video Tutorials:

Repurpose recorded webinars or live sessions into standalone video tutorials or series. Edit and enhance video content with captions, graphics, and animations to improve accessibility and engagement on platforms like YouTube or Vimeo.

3. eBooks into Blog Series:

Break down comprehensive eBooks or guides into a series of blog posts or articles. Each post can delve into specific chapters or sections, offering condensed insights and encouraging readers to explore the full eBook for more in-depth knowledge.

4. Podcast Episodes into Transcripts or Articles:

Transcribe podcast episodes and repurpose them into written articles, blog posts, or downloadable PDFs. Optimize transcripts with relevant keywords for SEO and provide alternative formats for audiences who prefer reading over listening.

5. Infographics into Slideshares:

Transform data-rich infographics into engaging slideshows or presentations using platforms like SlideShare. Summarize key findings, insights, or tips visually and include links back to the original infographic for deeper exploration.

6. Case Studies into Email Campaigns:

Adapt detailed case studies or customer success stories into email campaigns or newsletters. Highlight challenges, solutions, and results to demonstrate expertise and build credibility among subscribers interested in real-world examples.

7. Live Streams into Blog Posts:

Convert live streams, Q&A sessions, or AMA (Ask Me Anything) sessions into blog posts or articles. Summarize discussions, key takeaways, and audience interactions to provide valuable content in a written format.

8. Whitepapers into Webinars:

Transform research-driven whitepapers or reports into live or recorded webinars. Present findings, insights, and implications in an interactive format, allowing participants to engage with experts and ask questions in real-time.

9. FAQs into Social Media Stories:

Use frequently asked questions (FAQs) from customer support or website inquiries to create engaging social media stories or Instagram carousels. Address common queries, provide quick tips, or share customer testimonials to foster interaction and engagement.

10. User-Generated Content into Campaigns:

Curate and repurpose user-generated content (UGC), such as customer reviews, photos, or testimonials, into promotional campaigns or social media content. Showcase authentic experiences and encourage community participation and advocacy.

11. Blog Comments into Follow-up Content:

Turn insightful comments or discussions from blog posts into follow-up content pieces. Expand on specific topics, address reader feedback, or provide additional resources to continue the conversation and deepen engagement.

12. Evergreen Content Updates and Refreshes:

Regularly update and refresh evergreen content pieces with new statistics, examples, or developments. Republish updated versions to maintain relevance, improve SEO performance, and attract returning visitors seeking updated information.

Content repurposing allows businesses to maximize the value of their existing content investments, reach broader audiences across different platforms, and reinforce key messages through various formats. By strategically repurposing content, organizations can extend the content lifecycle, drive engagement, and achieve greater overall impact in their content marketing efforts.

6.3 User-Generated Content

User-generated content (UGC) refers to any form of content, such as images, videos, testimonials, reviews, or social media posts, created and shared by users or customers rather than brands or marketers themselves. UGC has become a valuable asset for businesses across various industries due to its authenticity, credibility, and ability to foster community engagement. Here are the key aspects and benefits of leveraging user-generated content:

1. Authenticity and Trustworthiness:

User-generated content is perceived as more authentic and trustworthy because it comes directly from real customers or users. It reflects genuine experiences, opinions, and perspectives, which can resonate strongly with potential customers.

2. Social Proof and Influence:

UGC serves as powerful social proof that influences purchasing decisions. Positive reviews, testimonials, or photos shared by satisfied customers can persuade others to trust your brand, products, or services, leading to increased conversion rates and sales.

3. Enhanced Engagement and Interaction:

Encouraging users to create and share content related to your brand fosters greater engagement and interaction. It creates a sense of community and encourages user participation, building stronger relationships and loyalty over time.

4. Cost-Effective Content Creation:

Leveraging UGC reduces the need for brands to create all content themselves, saving time and resources. User-generated content is often freely given or acquired through incentives such as contests or rewards, making it a cost-effective strategy for content creation.

5. Diversification of Content Types:

UGC provides a diverse range of content types beyond traditional marketing materials. It includes photos, videos, stories, reviews, and creative interpretations that showcase different aspects of your products or services from unique perspectives.

6. SEO Benefits and Visibility:

Incorporating UGC into your digital marketing strategy can improve search engine optimization (SEO) by generating organic content and backlinks. User-generated reviews and discussions contribute to fresh content updates and enhance your website's relevance and authority.

7. Community Building and Advocacy:

UGC helps build a sense of community around your brand by encouraging customers to share their experiences and connect with like-minded individuals. It fosters advocacy as satisfied customers become advocates who promote your brand organically to their networks.

8. Legal and Ethical Considerations:

Ensure compliance with legal guidelines and obtain consent from users before repurposing their content. Respect privacy rights and intellectual property laws when sharing or repurposing UGC to protect both your brand and the rights of content creators.

9. Monitoring and Moderation:

Implement systems to monitor and moderate UGC to maintain quality, relevance, and brand alignment. Engage with users, respond to comments, and address any concerns or negative feedback promptly to uphold a positive brand image.

10. Campaigns and Promotions:

Create campaigns or promotions that encourage UGC participation, such as photo contests, hashtag campaigns, or user-generated reviews. Provide incentives or rewards to motivate users to create and share content aligned with your brand values and marketing objectives.

Leveraging user-generated content effectively can significantly enhance your digital marketing efforts by tapping into the authentic voices and experiences of your customers. By encouraging UGC, brands can build trust, drive engagement, and amplify their brand reach through compelling and relatable content created by their community.

6.4 Interactive Content Ideas

Interactive content engages users actively, encouraging participation and creating memorable experiences that can drive higher levels of engagement and interaction. Here are some creative ideas for interactive content that businesses can incorporate into their digital marketing strategies:

1. **Quizzes and Assessments:**

Create interactive quizzes or assessments related to your industry, products, or services. Offer personalized results or recommendations based on user responses to increase engagement and provide value.

2. **Polls and Surveys:**

Conduct polls or surveys to gather insights, opinions, or feedback from your audience. Share results and insights with participants to foster transparency and encourage continued engagement.

3. **Calculators and Tools:**

Develop online calculators or interactive tools that help users estimate costs, savings, or benefits related to your products or services. Provide actionable insights or customized reports based on user inputs.

4. **Interactive Infographics:**

Transform static infographics into interactive formats that allow users to explore data points, toggle between different views, or click for additional information. Interactive infographics enhance visual storytelling and engagement.

5. Virtual Tours or 360° Experiences:

Offer virtual tours or 360° experiences of physical locations, products, or services. Allow users to navigate through immersive environments, showcasing key features or benefits dynamically and interactively.

6. Interactive Video Content:

Create interactive videos that allow viewers to choose their own path or storyline based on decision points within the video. Incorporate clickable hotspots, quizzes, or interactive overlays to enhance viewer engagement.

7. Contests and Challenges:

Host interactive contests or challenges that encourage user participation and creativity. Examples include photo contests, caption challenges, or user-generated content challenges with voting mechanisms.

8. Interactive eBooks or Flipbooks:

Develop interactive eBooks or flipbooks with multimedia elements, clickable links, embedded videos, and interactive content such as quizzes or simulations. Offer a dynamic reading experience that keeps users engaged.

9. Interactive Webinars or Workshops:

Conduct live or recorded interactive webinars or workshops where participants can ask questions, participate in polls or quizzes, and engage with presenters or guest speakers in real-time.

10. Gamification Elements:

Integrate gamification elements such as leaderboards, badges, or rewards into your interactive content to incentivize participation and increase motivation. Encourage competition and achievement to drive ongoing engagement.

11. Augmented Reality (AR) Experiences:

Develop AR experiences that allow users to interact with virtual objects or visualize products in their real-world environment. AR enhances engagement by providing immersive and interactive experiences.

12. Interactive Email Campaigns:

Embed interactive elements such as surveys, quizzes, or clickable images within email campaigns to increase engagement and encourage recipients to interact directly from their inboxes.

Implementing interactive content ideas can enrich your digital marketing strategy by capturing attention, encouraging active participation, and fostering deeper engagement with your audience. Tailor interactive experiences to align with your brand objectives, audience preferences, and desired outcomes to maximize impact and achieve marketing goals effectively.

6.5 Building a Content Calendar

A content calendar is a strategic tool that helps businesses plan, organize, and schedule their content creation and distribution efforts over a specified period. Building an effective content calendar ensures consistency, alignment with marketing objectives, and the timely delivery of valuable content to your audience. Here's how to build a comprehensive content calendar:

1. **Define Your Content Goals and Objectives:**

Identify overarching content marketing goals, such as increasing brand awareness, driving traffic, generating leads, or boosting engagement. Align content themes and topics with these objectives to ensure relevance and effectiveness.

2. **Conduct Audience Research:**

Understand your target audience's preferences, behaviors, and content consumption habits. Segment your audience based on demographics, interests, and purchasing intent to tailor content that resonates with their needs and preferences.

3. Choose Content Types and Formats:

Select a variety of content types and formats that align with your audience preferences and marketing goals. Consider blog posts, videos, infographics, eBooks, podcasts, webinars, case studies, and more to diversify your content strategy.

4. Brainstorm Content Ideas and Topics:

Generate a list of potential content ideas and topics based on keyword research, industry trends, customer FAQs, and seasonal themes. Ensure a balance of evergreen content and timely topics to maintain relevance.

5. Create a Content Calendar Template:

Use a spreadsheet, project management tool, or dedicated content calendar software to create a template. Include columns for content title, type/format, publication date, author, status, and any relevant notes or links.

6. Establish Content Themes and Pillars:

Define content themes or pillars that reflect key aspects of your brand and resonate with your target audience. Organize content around these themes to maintain consistency and reinforce brand messaging.

7. Assign Responsibilities and Deadlines:

Assign roles and responsibilities to team members involved in content creation, editing, design, and promotion. Set clear deadlines for each stage of content production to ensure timely delivery and accountability.

8. Incorporate SEO and Keyword Strategy:

Integrate SEO best practices into your content calendar by aligning topics with relevant keywords and search queries. Plan content clusters or series around core topics to improve search engine visibility and organic traffic.

9. Include Promotion and Distribution Plans:

Plan how and where each piece of content will be promoted and distributed across channels such as social media, email newsletters, blogs, and third-party platforms. Schedule promotional activities to maximize reach and engagement.

10. Review and Update Regularly:

Regularly review and update your content calendar to reflect changes in business priorities, industry trends, or audience preferences. Adjust publishing schedules and content themes as needed to optimize performance and effectiveness.

11. Measure and Analyze Results:

Track key performance indicators (KPIs) such as traffic, engagement, conversions, and ROI for each piece of content. Use analytics tools to assess content performance, identify top-performing assets, and inform future content decisions.

12. Stay Flexible and Agile:

Remain adaptable to unforeseen events or opportunities that may require adjustments to your content calendar. Maintain flexibility to capitalize on emerging trends or address timely issues while staying aligned with long-term objectives.

Building and maintaining a content calendar enables businesses to streamline content production, enhance consistency, and maximize the impact of their content marketing efforts. By implementing a structured approach to content planning and scheduling, organizations can effectively engage their audience, drive meaningful interactions, and achieve their marketing goals efficiently.

Chapter 7: Measuring Content Success

Measuring content success is essential for evaluating the effectiveness of your content marketing efforts, optimizing strategies, and achieving your business objectives. It involves assessing various metrics and KPIs to determine how well your content performs in engaging your audience, driving traffic, and contributing to overall business goals. Here's a comprehensive approach to measuring content success:

1. Define Key Objectives and Goals:

Clearly define specific objectives and goals for each piece of content or campaign. Align these goals with broader business objectives such as brand awareness, lead generation, customer retention, or sales conversion.

2. Identify Relevant Metrics and KPIs:

Select metrics and key performance indicators (KPIs) that align with your content goals. Examples include website traffic, page views, time on page, bounce rate, social shares, email open rates, conversion rates, and customer engagement metrics.

3. Use Analytics Tools:

Utilize analytics tools such as Google Analytics, social media insights, email marketing platforms, and CRM systems to track and measure content performance. Set up custom dashboards and reports to monitor KPIs regularly.

4. Track Audience Engagement:

Measure audience engagement metrics such as likes, comments, shares, retweets, and mentions across different content channels. Assess the level of interaction and participation to gauge content resonance and impact.

5. Evaluate SEO Performance:

Monitor SEO metrics including keyword rankings, organic search traffic, backlinks generated, and domain authority improvements. Analyze how well your content performs in driving organic visibility and search engine rankings.

6. Assess Conversion Rates:

Measure conversion rates associated with your content, such as lead generation form submissions, email sign-ups, demo requests, or online purchases. Analyze how effectively content moves users through the conversion funnel.

7. Analyze Content Reach and Amplification:

Evaluate the reach and amplification of your content across different channels. Track metrics such as reach, impressions, shares, and mentions to understand how widely your content is distributed and discussed.

8. Calculate ROI and Cost Efficiency:

Calculate the return on investment (ROI) of your content marketing efforts by comparing the costs incurred (e.g., production, promotion) with the outcomes achieved (e.g., revenue generated, cost per lead). Determine the cost efficiency of your content initiatives.

9. Compare Performance Over Time:

Compare content performance metrics over time to identify trends, patterns, and seasonality. Measure improvements or declines in performance to optimize content strategies and tactics accordingly.

10. Gather Qualitative Feedback:

Collect qualitative feedback from your audience through surveys, polls, or direct feedback mechanisms. Use insights to understand audience preferences, perceptions, and sentiments toward your content.

11. Benchmark against Competitors:

Benchmark your content performance against industry peers or competitors. Analyze their content strategies, engagement levels, and audience response to identify opportunities for differentiation and improvement.

12. Iterate and Optimize Content Strategies:

Use data-driven insights to iterate and optimize your content strategies. Adjust content formats, topics, distribution channels, and promotional tactics based on performance metrics and audience feedback.

By systematically measuring content success using a combination of quantitative metrics, qualitative insights, and comparative analysis, businesses can refine their content marketing strategies, enhance audience engagement, and achieve meaningful business outcomes. Continuously monitor and adapt your approach to stay aligned with evolving trends and audience preferences in the dynamic digital landscape.

7.1 Key Performance Indicators (KPIs) for Content

Key Performance Indicators (KPIs) for content are metrics used to measure the effectiveness, impact, and success of your content marketing efforts. These KPIs help businesses assess how well their content performs in achieving specific goals and objectives. Here are essential KPIs to consider when measuring content performance:

1. Website Traffic:

Measure the total number of visitors to your website attributed to specific pieces of content. Track overall traffic volume and identify which content drives the most visits.

2. Unique Visitors:

Evaluate the number of distinct individuals who visit your website, providing insights into new audience acquisition and reach.

3. Page Views:

Count the total number of times a page or piece of content is viewed on your website. Monitor which pages attract the highest views and engagement.

4. Average Time on Page:

Assess the average duration visitors spend on a page or content piece. Longer times often indicate higher engagement and interest.

5. Bounce Rate:

Measure the percentage of visitors who navigate away from your site after viewing only one page. A lower bounce rate typically signifies content relevance and engagement.

6. Conversion Rate:

Track the percentage of visitors who complete a desired action, such as signing up for a newsletter, downloading a whitepaper, or making a purchase.

7. Lead Generation:

Evaluate the number of leads generated through content, such as inquiries, form submissions, or registrations for events or webinars.

8. Social Media Engagement:

Monitor likes, shares, comments, and retweets across social media platforms. Assess audience interaction and content amplification.

9. Email Engagement:

Analyze email open rates, click-through rates (CTR), and conversion rates for email campaigns featuring content-driven messaging.

10. SEO Performance:

Track keyword rankings, organic search traffic, backlinks acquired, and domain authority improvements resulting from content efforts.

11. Return on Investment (ROI):

Calculate the financial return generated from content marketing activities relative to the costs incurred (e.g., production, promotion).

12. Customer Retention and Loyalty:

Measure customer retention rates and the impact of content on customer satisfaction and loyalty over time.

13. Brand Awareness and Perception:

Assess changes in brand awareness, perception, and sentiment influenced by content initiatives.

14. Content Amplification:

Gauge the reach and amplification of content through shares, mentions, and referrals, indicating its viral potential and impact.

15. Audience Engagement Metrics:

Evaluate metrics like session duration, interaction rate, comments per post, or shares per post to gauge active engagement and content resonance.

Selecting the right KPIs depends on your specific content goals and objectives. Regularly monitor and analyze these metrics to refine your content strategy, optimize performance, and drive meaningful business outcomes in alignment with your overall marketing efforts.

7.2 Using Analytics to Track Performance

Analytics tools play a crucial role in tracking and measuring the performance of your content marketing efforts. By leveraging analytics effectively, businesses can gain valuable insights into audience behavior, content effectiveness, and overall campaign success. Here's how to use analytics to track content performance:

1. Set Up Goals and Metrics:

Define specific goals and key performance indicators (KPIs) aligned with your content marketing objectives. Establish clear metrics such as website traffic, conversion rates, engagement metrics, and ROI to measure success.

2. Use Google Analytics (or Similar Tools):

Implement Google Analytics to monitor website traffic, user behavior, and content performance. Track metrics such as page views, unique visitors, average time on page, bounce rate, and goal completions.

3. Track Audience Behavior:

Analyze user behavior flow to understand how visitors navigate through your site and interact with content. Identify popular content paths, drop-off points, and conversion funnels to optimize user experience.

4. Monitor Content Engagement:

Measure engagement metrics such as likes, shares, comments, and social media interactions. Use social media analytics tools to track audience engagement across platforms and assess content amplification.

5. Assess SEO Performance:

Monitor SEO metrics including keyword rankings, organic search traffic, backlinks, and domain authority. Use tools like SEMrush, Moz, or Ahrefs to track keyword performance and identify opportunities for optimization.

6. Analyze Email Campaign Metrics:

Evaluate email campaign performance using email marketing platforms. Track metrics such as open rates, click-through rates (CTR), conversion rates, and subscriber behavior to optimize content relevance and delivery.

7. Utilize Content Performance Reports:

Generate custom reports or dashboards to consolidate and analyze content performance data. Use visualizations to identify trends, patterns, and correlations that impact content effectiveness and audience engagement.

8. Implement UTM Parameters:

Use UTM parameters in URLs to track the effectiveness of specific campaigns, channels, or content pieces in Google Analytics. Monitor campaign attribution and performance across different marketing channels.

9. A/B Testing and Experimentation:

Conduct A/B tests or experiments to compare different content variations, headlines, calls-to-action (CTAs), or layouts. Use analytics to measure performance differences and identify high-performing content elements.

10. Benchmark Against Industry Standards:

Compare your content performance metrics against industry benchmarks and competitors. Gain insights into market trends, audience preferences, and opportunities for improvement or differentiation.

11. Regularly Review and Optimize:

Continuously review analytics data to identify underperforming content, optimize strategies, and capitalize on high-performing content. Adjust content tactics based on data-driven insights to maximize ROI and achieve marketing goals.

12. Generate Insights and Actionable Recommendations:

Translate analytics data into actionable recommendations and strategic insights. Use findings to refine content strategies, allocate resources effectively, and drive continuous improvement in content marketing initiatives.

By leveraging analytics tools and data-driven insights, businesses can measure, analyze, and optimize content performance effectively. Monitoring key metrics and user behavior empowers marketers to make informed decisions, improve engagement, and achieve measurable results in their content marketing efforts.

7.3 A/B Testing for Content Optimization

A/B testing, also known as split testing, is a valuable technique used in content marketing to compare two versions of a webpage, email, or other content elements to determine which performs better. By systematically testing variations, businesses can optimize content for higher engagement, conversions, and overall effectiveness. Here's how to effectively implement A/B testing for content optimization:

1. **Define Your Objective:**

Clearly define the goal of your A/B test, such as increasing click-through rates (CTR), improving conversion rates, reducing bounce rates, or enhancing user engagement.

2. **Identify Elements to Test:**

Select specific content elements or variables to test, such as headlines, call-to-action (CTA) buttons, images, layouts, colors, copywriting styles, or overall content structure.

3. **Develop Hypotheses:**

Formulate hypotheses based on insights from audience research, analytics data, or industry best practices. Predict which variation you believe will perform better and why.

4. Create Variations:

Develop two versions (A and B) of your content, each differing in one specific element or variable. Ensure changes are significant enough to generate measurable differences in performance.

5. Implement Testing Tools:

Utilize A/B testing tools or platforms such as Google Optimize, Optimizely, or HubSpot to conduct experiments. Set up test parameters, including sample size, duration, and traffic allocation between variants.

6. Run Experiments Concurrently:

Simultaneously present variant A to one segment of your audience and variant B to another segment. Ensure tests run under similar conditions to minimize external factors influencing results.

7. Measure Performance Metrics:

Track key performance indicators (KPIs) relevant to your objective. Monitor metrics such as CTR, conversion rates, engagement rates, bounce rates, or time spent on the page for each variant.

8. Analyze Results Statistically:

Evaluate test results using statistical significance to determine the winning variant. Tools often provide statistical confidence levels (e.g., p-values) indicating whether differences in performance are significant.

9. Draw Insights and Learnings:

Analyze insights gained from the A/B test results. Identify which content variant outperformed and understand why. Document findings to apply learnings to future content optimization strategies.

10. Implement Winning Variation:

Implement the winning variation identified through A/B testing as the new standard. Update content across relevant channels based on insights gained to maximize performance and achieve desired goals.

11. Iterate and Test Continuously:

Continuously iterate and refine content elements based on ongoing A/B tests. Test additional variables or hypotheses to further optimize content performance and maintain competitive advantage.

12. Document and Share Findings:

Document A/B testing procedures, results, and recommendations. Share findings with stakeholders, content creators, and marketing teams to foster a culture of data-driven decision-making and continuous improvement.

A/B testing empowers content marketers to make informed decisions, improve audience engagement, and achieve measurable results by systematically comparing and optimizing content variations. By embracing a structured approach to testing and experimentation, businesses can enhance content effectiveness, drive conversions, and ultimately, achieve their content marketing objectives more effectively.

7.4 Understanding Conversion Rates

Conversion rates are a critical metric in digital marketing that measures the percentage of visitors who complete a desired action or goal on a website, landing page, or within a marketing campaign. Understanding conversion rates is essential for evaluating the effectiveness of marketing efforts and optimizing strategies to achieve business objectives. Here's a comprehensive overview of conversion rates:

1. Definition of Conversion Rates:

Conversion rates represent the percentage of website visitors who take a specific action that aligns with your business goals. Common conversions include making a purchase, filling out a form, signing up for a newsletter, downloading a resource, or completing a registration.

2. Types of Conversions:

- **Macro Conversions**: These are primary actions directly tied to revenue or business objectives, such as completing a purchase or requesting a demo.
- **Micro Conversions**: These are secondary actions that indicate progress towards a macro conversion, such as signing up for a free trial, adding items to a cart, or subscribing to a blog.

3. Importance of Conversion Rates:

Conversion rates indicate the effectiveness of your marketing campaigns, website usability, and content relevance in persuading visitors to take action. They directly impact revenue generation, customer acquisition costs, and return on investment (ROI).

4. Calculating Conversion Rates:

The conversion rate is calculated using the formula:

$$\text{Conversion Rate} = \frac{\text{Number of Conversions}}{\text{Number of Sessions}} \times 100$$

Number of Conversions: Total number of desired actions completed.

Number of Sessions: Total number of visits or sessions to your website or landing page during the same period.

5. **Factors Influencing Conversion Rates:**

- **Website Design and User Experience**: Navigation ease, page load times, and intuitive layout affect user engagement and conversion rates.
- **Content Relevance and Quality**: Content that addresses user needs, provides value, and aligns with audience interests can increase conversion rates.
- **Call-to-Action (CTA) Effectiveness**: Clear, compelling CTAs that guide users toward desired actions are crucial for improving conversion rates.
- **Traffic Sources and Quality**: Targeted traffic from relevant channels tends to have higher conversion rates compared to non-targeted or low-quality traffic.
- **Trust and Credibility**: Testimonials, reviews, security badges, and transparent policies can enhance trust and positively impact conversion rates.

6. **Benchmarking and Goals:**

Benchmark conversion rates against industry standards and historical data to set realistic goals. Continuous optimization based on data-driven insights helps improve conversion rates over time.

7. **Monitoring and Optimization Strategies:**

Regularly monitor conversion rates using analytics tools. Implement A/B testing, optimize landing pages, CTAs, and content based on performance data to increase conversion rates.

8. Conversion Rate Optimization (CRO):

CRO involves systematic efforts to improve conversion rates through iterative testing, analysis, and refinement of website elements and marketing strategies. It focuses on maximizing the efficiency of every visitor interaction.

9. Attribution and Tracking:

Use attribution models to track and attribute conversions to specific marketing channels or touchpoints. Understand the customer journey and which interactions contribute most to conversions.

10. Continuous Improvement:

Embrace a culture of continuous improvement by leveraging data insights, customer feedback, and industry trends to refine strategies, enhance user experience, and optimize conversion rates effectively.

Understanding and optimizing conversion rates are fundamental to achieving marketing goals and driving business growth. By focusing on improving user experience, delivering relevant content, and refining conversion funnel strategies, businesses can increase conversions and maximize the impact of their digital marketing efforts.

7.5 Adapting Strategies Based on Analytics

Analytics provide valuable insights into the performance of your marketing efforts, allowing you to make informed decisions and optimize strategies for better results. Here's how to effectively adapt your strategies based on analytics data:

1. **Review Key Performance Indicators (KPIs):**

Monitor KPIs such as website traffic, conversion rates, engagement metrics, bounce rates, and ROI regularly using analytics tools like Google Analytics, Adobe Analytics, or other relevant platforms.

2. **Identify Trends and Patterns:**

Analyze analytics data to identify trends, patterns, and correlations related to content performance, audience behavior, and campaign effectiveness. Look for insights that indicate what is working well and what needs improvement.

3. **Understand Audience Behavior:**

Gain insights into how your target audience interacts with your content and navigates through your website. Identify popular pages, entry points, exit points, and content consumption patterns to optimize user experience.

4.   Evaluate Content Performance:

Assess the performance of individual content pieces, campaigns, or channels based on metrics such as page views, time on page, shares, comments, and conversion rates. Identify high-performing content and areas for improvement.

5.   Segment and Analyze Audience Data:

Segment your audience based on demographics, behavior, interests, and acquisition channels. Tailor content strategies and messaging to better meet the needs and preferences of different audience segments.

6.   Conduct A/B Testing and Experiments:

Use A/B testing to experiment with different variations of content, CTAs, layouts, or campaign elements. Test hypotheses derived from analytics insights to determine which variations drive better performance.

7.   Optimize Conversion Funnel:

Identify bottlenecks or barriers in your conversion funnel by analyzing drop-off points and abandonment rates. Optimize landing pages, CTAs, forms, and checkout processes to reduce friction and improve conversion rates.

8.   Adjust Marketing Tactics:

Based on analytics findings, adjust your marketing tactics and channel mix. Allocate resources to channels and campaigns that drive the highest ROI and reallocate budget from underperforming channels.

9.   Personalize Content and Messaging:

Leverage audience data to personalize content and messaging. Deliver relevant content recommendations, personalized offers, and targeted communications to enhance engagement and conversion rates.

10. Monitor Competitor Performance:

Benchmark your performance against industry peers and competitors using competitive analysis tools. Identify opportunities and trends that can inform adjustments to your strategies and tactics.

11. Implement Data-Driven Decisions:

Use analytics data to make data-driven decisions backed by insights rather than assumptions. Continuously monitor and iterate your strategies based on real-time performance data and market dynamics.

12. Measure Impact and Iterate:

Measure the impact of strategy adjustments on key metrics and KPIs. Iterate and refine your strategies based on performance outcomes to optimize long-term success and achieve business objectives.

By adapting your strategies based on analytics data, you can optimize marketing efforts, improve campaign effectiveness, and achieve better outcomes. Embrace a proactive approach to leveraging data insights to drive continuous improvement and innovation in your marketing initiatives.

Chapter 8: The Future of Content Writing

The landscape of content writing is continually evolving, driven by technological advancements, shifting consumer behaviors, and emerging trends in digital marketing. As we look ahead, several key factors are shaping the future of content writing:

1. Artificial Intelligence and Automation:

AI-powered tools and automation are revolutionizing content creation, optimization, and personalization. Natural Language Processing (NLP) and machine learning algorithms enable marketers to generate data-driven insights, automate content distribution, and deliver personalized experiences at scale.

2. Visual and Interactive Content:

Visual content formats such as videos, infographics, and interactive elements are gaining prominence. They enhance engagement, convey complex information effectively, and cater to the preferences of today's multimedia-savvy audiences.

3. Voice Search and Conversational AI:

The rise of voice search and smart assistants (e.g., Siri, Alexa) is influencing content strategies. Optimizing content for voice queries and conversational AI requires natural language understanding, concise answers, and structured data markup.

4. Content Personalization:

Personalized content experiences are becoming essential to engage and retain audiences. Leveraging data analytics, marketers can deliver tailored content recommendations, personalized offers, and dynamic content based on user preferences and behaviors.

5. E-A-T and Trustworthiness:

Expertise, Authority, and Trustworthiness (E-A-T) are critical factors for content credibility and search engine rankings. Emphasizing authoritative sources, expert opinions, and transparent content practices will continue to be paramount.

6. User-Generated Content and Community Building:

User-generated content (UGC) plays a pivotal role in building brand trust and authenticity. Encouraging user participation, reviews, and testimonials fosters community engagement and amplifies brand storytelling.

7. Sustainability and Ethical Content Practices:

Consumers are increasingly prioritizing brands that uphold sustainability and ethical practices. Content that reflects corporate social responsibility (CSR), diversity, equity, and inclusion (DEI) initiatives will resonate with socially-conscious audiences.

8. SEO and Content Strategy Integration:

SEO remains foundational for content visibility and organic traffic. Integrating SEO best practices, such as keyword optimization, structured data markup, and mobile-friendly content, will continue to drive search engine rankings and visibility.

9. Content Distribution and Omnichannel Marketing:

Effective content distribution across multiple channels (e.g., social media, email, and blogs) is essential for reaching diverse audiences. Omnichannel marketing strategies that deliver consistent messaging and seamless user experiences will be pivotal.

10. Continuous Learning and Adaptation:

Content writers must embrace lifelong learning and adaptability. Staying abreast of industry trends, consumer insights, and technological innovations will empower content creators to innovate and stay competitive in a dynamic digital landscape.

As content writing evolves, embracing technological advancements, prioritizing user experience, and maintaining authenticity will be key to driving engagement, fostering brand loyalty, and achieving marketing success in the future. Adapting strategies to meet evolving consumer expectations and industry trends will position businesses to thrive amidst digital transformation.

8.1 Emerging Trends in Content Marketing

Content marketing continues to evolve rapidly, shaped by technological advancements, changing consumer behaviors, and innovations in digital media. Emerging trends are transforming how brands create, distribute, and optimize content to engage audiences effectively. Here are key emerging trends in content marketing:

1. Video Content Dominance:

Video content is becoming increasingly popular across platforms like YouTube, TikTok, and Instagram. Brands are leveraging short-form videos, live streaming, and interactive video formats to engage audiences authentically and convey compelling brand stories.

2. AI-Powered Content Creation:

Artificial Intelligence (AI) is revolutionizing content creation processes. AI tools equipped with Natural Language Processing (NLP) capabilities can generate personalized content, automate content production, and optimize content performance based on data-driven insights.

3. Voice Search Optimization:

With the rise of smart assistants like Siri, Alexa, and Google Assistant, optimizing content for voice search is crucial. Marketers are focusing on creating conversational content, using long-tail keywords, and enhancing structured data to improve visibility in voice search results.

4. Interactive and Immersive Experiences:

Interactive content formats such as quizzes, polls, AR/VR experiences, and gamification are enhancing user engagement. These formats encourage active participation, increase time spent on content, and foster deeper connections with brands.

5. Personalization at Scale:

Personalized content experiences tailored to individual preferences and behaviors are driving engagement and conversions. Marketers are using data analytics and AI-driven insights to deliver personalized recommendations, dynamic content, and targeted messaging across channels.

6. Sustainability and Ethical Branding:

Consumers are increasingly prioritizing brands that demonstrate sustainability practices and ethical values. Content that highlights corporate social responsibility (CSR), environmental initiatives, and ethical business practices resonates with socially conscious audiences.

7. Long-Form and Evergreen Content:

Long-form content such as comprehensive guides, whitepapers, and in-depth articles is gaining traction. Evergreen content that remains relevant over time continues to attract organic traffic, build authority, and support SEO efforts.

8. User-Generated Content (UGC) and Community Engagement:

UGC, including customer reviews, testimonials, and social media content, plays a pivotal role in building trust and authenticity. Brands are fostering community engagement, encouraging user participation, and amplifying brand advocacy through UGC campaigns.

9. Omnichannel Content Strategies:

Omnichannel marketing approaches that deliver consistent messaging across multiple platforms (e.g., social media, email, and website) are essential for reaching diverse audiences. Seamless integration and personalized experiences across channels enhance brand visibility and customer engagement.

10. Data Privacy and Trust-Centric Marketing:

Amidst growing concerns about data privacy, brands are prioritizing transparent data practices and building trust with consumers. Content that emphasizes security measures, data protection policies, and respect for consumer privacy preferences enhances brand credibility.

11. Influencer Collaboration and Co-Creation:

Collaborating with influencers and industry experts to co-create content fosters authenticity and expands reach. Influencer partnerships enable brands to leverage niche audiences, build credibility, and drive engagement through authentic storytelling.

12. Agile Content Marketing and Real-Time Engagement:

Agile content strategies that respond to real-time trends and consumer insights are gaining prominence. Brands are leveraging social listening tools, monitoring trending topics, and adapting content in real time to stay relevant and engage with audiences effectively.

As content marketing continues to evolve, staying ahead of emerging trends, leveraging innovative technologies, and prioritizing audience-centric strategies will be crucial for brands seeking to create impactful and memorable content experiences. Embracing these trends enables brands to adapt to changing market dynamics, drive meaningful connections with consumers, and achieve sustainable growth in the digital era.

8.2 The Role of AI in Content Creation

Artificial Intelligence (AI) is transforming content creation processes, empowering marketers and content creators to enhance efficiency, personalize content, and optimize performance. Here's how AI is revolutionizing content creation:

1. **Automated Content Generation:**

AI-powered tools equipped with Natural Language Processing (NLP) capabilities can generate content at scale. From writing blog posts, and product descriptions, to social media captions, AI streamlines content creation processes, saving time and resources.

2. **Personalized Content Recommendations:**

AI analyzes user data and behavioral patterns to deliver personalized content recommendations. By understanding individual preferences and interests, AI algorithms suggest relevant articles, videos, or products, enhancing user engagement and satisfaction.

3. **Content Curation and Aggregation:**

AI algorithms curate and aggregate content from various sources based on specific topics or themes. This automated process ensures a steady flow of relevant content for websites, blogs, and social media channels, keeping audiences informed and engaged.

4. Language Translation and Localization:

AI-powered translation tools facilitate multilingual content creation and localization. By translating text accurately and maintaining context, AI helps brands reach global audiences effectively and expand their market presence.

5. SEO and Content Optimization:

AI analyzes search trends, keyword data, and user intent to optimize content for search engines. AI-driven tools recommend relevant keywords, suggest improvements in content structure, and enhance readability, improving SEO performance and visibility.

6. Natural Language Generation (NLG):

NLG technology enables AI to generate human-like text based on structured data inputs. This capability is utilized in creating reports, summaries, personalized emails, and other content formats that require clarity and coherence.

7. Content Performance Analytics:

AI algorithms analyze content performance metrics such as engagement rates, click-through rates (CTR), and conversion rates. By identifying patterns and insights from data, AI helps marketers understand what content resonates best with their audience and optimize future strategies.

8. Predictive Analytics for Content Strategy:

AI-driven predictive analytics forecast trends and consumer behavior, guiding content strategy development. By predicting content effectiveness and audience response, AI empowers marketers to proactively adapt strategies and stay ahead of the competition.

9. Enhanced User Experience (UX):

AI-powered chatbots and virtual assistants improve UX by providing instant responses to customer queries, personalized recommendations, and guiding users through content or product selections. This enhances engagement and fosters positive interactions with brands.

10. Creative Assistance and Ideation:

AI tools assist in brainstorming content ideas, generating creative concepts, and refining storytelling techniques. By analyzing data trends and consumer insights, AI inspires innovative content strategies that resonate with target audiences.

11. Ethical Considerations and Oversight:

Despite its benefits, AI in content creation raises ethical considerations such as transparency, bias detection, and adherence to privacy regulations. Brands need to implement responsible AI practices and maintain human oversight to ensure ethical content creation.

AI continues to evolve and redefine content creation processes, offering unprecedented opportunities for brands to deliver personalized, engaging, and impactful content experiences. By leveraging AI technologies effectively, marketers can optimize resources, drive audience engagement, and achieve sustainable growth in the digital era.

8.3 Voice Search Optimization

Voice search optimization is increasingly crucial in digital marketing strategies as consumers use voice-enabled devices like smartphones, smart speakers, and virtual assistants (e.g., Siri, Alexa, and Google Assistant) to search for information and make inquiries. Optimizing for voice search involves understanding user behavior, adapting content strategies, and implementing technical best practices to enhance visibility and engagement. Here's how businesses can effectively optimize for voice search:

1. **Understanding User Intent and Behavior:**

Voice search queries tend to be conversational and longer than text-based queries. Businesses must analyze common questions, phrases, and keywords used in voice searches to align content with user intent effectively.

2. **Long-Tail Keywords and Natural Language:**

Optimize content with long-tail keywords and phrases that mimic natural language patterns. Voice search queries often include question words (e.g., what, where, how), so incorporating these into content helps match user queries more closely.

3. Featured Snippets and Position Zero:

Aim to secure featured snippets or the position zero spot in search engine results pages (SERPs). These concise answers to user queries are often read aloud by virtual assistants, providing instant visibility and credibility.

4. Local SEO and Geo-Targeting:

Optimize for local intent by including location-specific keywords and phrases. Voice searches frequently include "near me" queries, making local SEO strategies essential for businesses targeting geographically relevant audiences.

5. Mobile-Friendly and Fast-Loading Content:

Ensure your website is mobile-friendly and optimized for fast loading speeds. Voice search users often access content on the go via mobile devices, and responsive design enhances user experience and reduces bounce rates.

6. Structured Data Markup:

Implement structured data markup (Schema.org) to provide search engines with context about your content. This helps search engines understand and index your content accurately, improving your chances of appearing in voice search results.

7. Natural Language Processing (NLP) and AI:

Leverage AI-driven tools and NLP technologies to understand user queries and generate content that matches search intent. AI can analyze data trends, predict user behavior, and optimize content for voice search effectively.

8. FAQ Pages and Conversational Content:

Create FAQ pages that address common questions related to your industry, products, or services. Structuring content in a conversational tone and anticipating user queries improves the chances of appearing in voice search results.

9. User Experience (UX) and Accessibility:

Prioritize user experience and accessibility across devices and platforms. Clear navigation, intuitive design, and accessible content formats enhance usability and engagement, improving voice search performance.

10. Monitor Performance and Adapt Strategies:

Regularly monitor analytics data to track performance metrics related to voice search optimization. Evaluate user engagement, traffic sources, and conversion rates to refine strategies and capitalize on emerging trends.

Voice search optimization is integral to enhancing brand visibility, engaging with audiences effectively, and staying competitive in the evolving digital landscape. By understanding user behavior, optimizing content for natural language queries, and leveraging technical SEO practices, businesses can position themselves for success in voice search-driven environments.

8.4 The Importance of Personalization

Personalization in marketing refers to tailoring content, products, and experiences to meet the specific needs and preferences of individual consumers. It plays a crucial role in enhancing customer satisfaction, driving engagement, and ultimately improving business outcomes. Here's why personalization is important in today's digital landscape:

1. Enhanced Customer Experience:

Personalized experiences make customers feel valued and understood. By delivering relevant content, product recommendations, and communications based on past behavior and preferences, brands can create seamless and enjoyable interactions.

2. Increased Engagement and Conversion Rates:

Personalization leads to higher engagement levels as personalized content resonates more effectively with individual interests. This targeted approach enhances click-through rates, reduces bounce rates, and ultimately increases conversion rates.

3. Building Customer Loyalty and Trust:

Tailoring experiences to individual preferences fosters stronger emotional connections with customers. Brands that consistently deliver personalized experiences demonstrate a commitment to understanding and meeting customer needs, building trust and loyalty over time.

4. Improved Customer Satisfaction and Retention:

By anticipating and fulfilling customer expectations through personalized offerings and communications, brands can improve overall satisfaction levels. Satisfied customers are more likely to become repeat buyers and advocates for the brand.

5. Driving Revenue Growth and ROI:

Personalization strategies contribute to revenue growth by increasing average order value and customer lifetime value. By delivering relevant product recommendations and upsell opportunities, brands can maximize sales opportunities and ROI.

6. Data-Driven Insights and Decision Making:

Personalization relies on data analytics to understand customer behaviors, preferences, and purchase patterns. By analyzing customer data, brands gain actionable insights that inform strategic decisions, marketing campaigns, and product development.

7. Competitive Advantage in the Market:

Brands that excel in personalization differentiate themselves from competitors. Personalized experiences set brands apart in a crowded marketplace, attracting and retaining customers who value customized interactions.

8. Adaptability to Consumer Expectations:

In an era where consumers expect tailored experiences, personalization demonstrates responsiveness to individual needs and preferences. Brands that adapt to evolving consumer expectations are better positioned for long-term success and growth.

9. Omnichannel and Cross-Channel Consistency:

Personalization across multiple channels, including websites, email, social media, and physical stores, ensures consistent messaging and experiences. Omnichannel personalization enhances brand visibility and strengthens customer relationships.

10. Ethical Considerations and Privacy Protection:

Maintaining ethical practices in data collection and usage is essential in personalization efforts. Respecting customer privacy preferences and adhering to data protection regulations (e.g., GDPR, CCPA) builds trust and credibility with consumers.

In conclusion, personalization is not just a trend but a strategic imperative for brands aiming to foster meaningful connections with customers, drive engagement, and achieve sustainable growth. By leveraging data-driven insights and adopting personalized marketing strategies, brands can create memorable experiences that resonate with individual preferences and expectations in the digital age.

8.5 Continuing Education and Skill Development

Continuing education and skill development are integral to personal and professional growth, particularly in fields that evolve rapidly like content writing and digital marketing. Here's why ongoing learning is crucial and how individuals can effectively develop their skills:

1. Keeping Pace with Industry Trends:

Industries, especially digital marketing and content writing, undergo frequent changes due to technological advancements and shifting consumer behaviors. Continuing education helps professionals stay updated with the latest trends, tools, and best practices.

2.   Enhancing Competence and Expertise:

Continuous learning allows individuals to deepen their knowledge and expand their skill set. By acquiring new skills such as SEO optimization, content strategy development, or social media marketing, professionals can enhance their competence and become subject matter experts.

3.   Adapting to Technological Advancements:

Technology evolves rapidly, influencing how content is created, distributed, and consumed. Learning new technologies and tools, such as AI-driven content generators or analytics platforms, enables professionals to leverage innovations effectively in their roles.

4.   Fostering Innovation and Creativity:

Education encourages creativity by exposing individuals to diverse perspectives, ideas, and approaches. By exploring new concepts and techniques, professionals can innovate in their content creation strategies and develop fresh, engaging content for audiences.

5.   Meeting Career Advancement Goals:

Continuing education plays a pivotal role in career progression and advancement. Upgrading skills in areas such as leadership, project management, or data analysis enhances employability and opens doors to higher-level roles and responsibilities.

6.   Networking and Collaboration Opportunities:

Educational programs, workshops, and conferences provide opportunities to network with industry peers, mentors, and thought leaders. Collaborating with others fosters knowledge sharing, builds professional relationships, and facilitates career growth.

7.   Adaptability to Market Demands:

Professionals who invest in ongoing education are better equipped to adapt to market demands and economic changes. They can pivot their skills to meet emerging needs, seize opportunities, and navigate challenges effectively in dynamic industries.

8.   Lifelong Learning Mindset:

Embracing a mindset of lifelong learning demonstrates a commitment to personal and professional development. It encourages individuals to seek continuous improvement, stay curious, and remain resilient in the face of evolving industry landscapes.

9.   Access to Online Learning Resources:

Online platforms offer a wealth of resources, including courses, webinars, tutorials, and certifications. Professionals can leverage these resources to acquire new skills at their own pace, regardless of location or schedule constraints.

10. Self-Reflection and Goal Setting:

Continuing education fosters self-reflection and goal setting by encouraging professionals to assess their strengths, areas for improvement and career aspirations. Setting clear learning objectives helps individuals prioritize their development efforts effectively.

In conclusion, continuing education and skill development are essential for content writers and digital marketers to thrive in competitive environments, innovate in their practices, and achieve long-term career success. By investing in continuous learning, professionals can stay ahead of industry trends, expand their capabilities, and deliver impactful results in their roles.

Conclusion

In this comprehensive guide to content writing, we have explored the essential principles and strategies for creating compelling, SEO-friendly content across various digital platforms. From understanding the fundamentals of content writing to mastering advanced techniques, this book has equipped you with the knowledge and skills necessary to excel in the dynamic field of digital marketing.

Effective content writing goes beyond mere words on a page; it is about connecting with your audience, delivering value, and driving meaningful actions. By implementing the strategies discussed in this guide—such as crafting engaging narratives, optimizing for search engines, and leveraging analytics for insights—you can enhance your content's visibility, engagement, and conversion rates.

Throughout our journey, we have emphasized the importance of understanding your audience's needs, preferences, and behaviors. Whether you are writing for websites, blogs, or social media platforms, tailoring your content to resonate with your target audience is key to building trust, fostering loyalty, and achieving business objectives.

As technology continues to evolve and consumer expectations evolve with it, staying adaptable and continuously learning are critical. Embrace new trends like AI-driven content creation, voice search optimization, and personalized marketing to stay ahead of the curve and deliver exceptional content experiences.

Remember, content writing is both an art and a science—a blend of creativity and strategy. It requires continuous refinement, experimentation, and a deep understanding of your brand's voice and identity. By staying curious, exploring new ideas, and refining your skills, you can consistently create content that captivates audiences and drives tangible results.

Whether you are just starting your journey in content writing or looking to refine your existing skills, this guide has provided you with a solid foundation to succeed. Keep experimenting, keep learning, and most importantly, keep writing with passion and purpose.

Here's to your success in mastering the art of content writing and achieving your digital marketing goals. Happy writing!

www.ingramcontent.com/pod-product-compliance
Lightning Source LLC
LaVergne TN
LVHW081527050326
832903LV00025B/1665